A Parent's Guide to 3rd Grade

A Parent's Guide to 3rd Grade

How to Ensure Your Child's Success

Ricki Winegardner

LEARNINGEXPRESS

NEW YORK

4|2001 GenFunds 15⁰⁰

Library of Congress Cataloging-in-Publication Data:

Winegardner, Ricki.

    A parent's guide to third grade/ by Ricki Winegardner.

        p. com.

    ISBN 1-57685-361-6

    1. Third Grade (Education)—United States. 2. Education, Primary—Parent

Participation—United States. I. Title.

    LB1571 3rd .W56 2001

    372.24'1—dc21

                         00-061216

Reprinted materials:

Copyright © 2000 National Center for Learning Disabilities, Inc; see page 131.

Copyright © 2000 The President's Challenge; see pages 40–41.

Printed in the United States of America

9 8 7 6 5 4 3 2 1

First Edition

For more information or to place an order, contact LearningExpress at:

900 Broadway

Suite 604

New York, NY 10003

Or visit us at:

    www.learnatest.com

Contents

Acknowledgments   vii

1
Welcome to 3rd Grade   1

Introduces the academic and social goals of third grade. Stresses the importance of parental involvement in a child's success.

2
What Your Child Is Learning in School   13

An overview for parents on what their children are learning in third grade in the core subjects: Reading/Language Arts, Writing, Math, Science, Social Studies, and the special subjects: Music, Computer Lab, Art, Physical Education, and Foreign Language.

3
How to Supplement
What Your Child Is Learning   49

Creative, easy, and effective ways for parents to help reinforce school lessons at home. Divided by subject for easy reference.

4
Your Child's Social Development   71

A briefing on the social skills taught in third grade. Describes the most common social problems in the third grade and shows parents how to help their child foster good social skills.

5

The 3rd-Grade Partnership:
You, Your Child, Your Child's Teacher 90

Stresses the importance of getting along with your child's teacher. Helps parents understand how success is dependent on the effort put in by all those involved.

6

The 3rd-Grade Problem Solver 106

Addresses all the common homework hassles in a question and answer format. Offers practical solutions to these problems and advice on how to determine how much you should help your child with homework.

7

On Gifted and Learning Disabled Children 122

Working with a gifted or learning-disabled child adds complexity to your role as a parent. This chapter gives you the facts and offers the best way of providing the necessary challenges or support for your child.

Resources:
The Best "Stuff" for 3rd Graders 139

A selective, annotated review of the best magazines, books, CD-ROMs, and websites for third graders and their parents.

Acknowledgments

FIRST and foremost, I would love to recognize those people who are my daily source of inspiration, knowledge, and strength.

My son, Seth, who killed the spider so that I was able to return to my keyboard.

My daughter, Sara, who reminded me that I needed a break every so often—if only to get her a drink.

My son, Ross, who often got the drink for Sara in my place, so that I would not have to move my atrophied self from the chair.

My husband, Darin, who, while I was stuck in my chair, mastered the culinary feat of preparing frozen pizzas.

There are wonderful people that I entrust my children to 180 days a year—the educators at our local schools. Thank you Pam Ott, Carolyn Kneas, Chris Shelley, and Sarah Peck. I am thankful to each of you for the time you spent talking with me, sharing materials, and even providing a quiet workplace for me on a busy afternoon! I am so thankful to not only call you "teacher," but to call you "friend." Our schools and communities are better because of you!

To the many parents who responded to my seemingly endless barrage of questions about their children, thank you! You were all so wonderfully candid!

I would be remiss if I did not mention my quirky friends and co-workers. Thanks Kelly for strongly encouraging me to join you at the gym. Those workouts stretched my atrophied muscles. Thanks Steve for sometimes talking me out of joining Kelly at the gym so that I could enjoy burgers and fries. And thanks Kevin for listening to my brain dumps. To all of you, your support was key! Brenda, Faith, Tammy and Janice, how would I have managed without your constant support? May we always stir the soup together!

A special thank you to the behind-the-scenes staff for your tireless efforts. Sandy Gade and Jennifer Farthing, you are truly the forces who brought this project to fruition!

There are so many others who provided support and guidance, and therefore helped this book become a reality. To each of you, my deepest gratitude.

Welcome to 3rd Grade

SUMMER vacation is coming to a close and your days are filled with buying school supplies, new clothes and shoes, and enjoying the last few days at the pool. Perhaps you are squeezing in one last weekend trip to the beach or museum before the yellow school busses fill the streets carrying fresh and eager faces back to school. Many parents find that as the dog days of summer wane, their anxiety about the impending school year grows.

As you network with your friends and co-workers, you will hear about how demanding one teacher is, how compassionate another teacher is, how long or short the bus ride is, and just how different third grade is from the other grades your child has completed thus far. Perhaps another parent will roll her eyes as though she knows a deep dark secret when you divulge which teacher your child has for the impending third grade. Yet another parent will look wistfully, wishing that his third grader would have your child's teacher. All of these mixed signals; all of this uncertainty, and in the midst of it all is a knob-by-kneed little person missing two front teeth.

You may also worry because during an open house at school, you noticed that the third-grade rooms did not seem to be as colorful or playful as the second-grade rooms. Did you also notice that the miniature tables and matching red plastic chairs of the earlier school years are gone? Now the desks are lined up in rows, with attached chairs, or larger detached chairs all waiting like posts for a squadron of third-grade soldiers to take their place behind them. You wonder if you should send the oversized shirt that, when put on backwards becomes a craft smock, to school this year. I remember wondering if they still would use paste and construction paper in the classroom this year.

There may be some new concerns, things that you never worried about before. Because you are a veteran parent of a school-age child, you know some of the other children who will also be attending third grade, or for that matter, any of the other grades. You may find yourself stressed out because one of the children assigned to the same class as your third grader is showing signs of being a bully. First and foremost, a nagging internal voice cries out to you, "How will my child do this year? Will she be ok? Gosh, she is growing up so fast!"

SIGNS OF ACADEMIC DIFFICULTY

Your child will be learning a lot this year, and he may be having some problems. Although these problems might just be temporary, they may be a sign of a learning disability or a skill deficiency. These deficiencies are often accompanied by warning signs, which may include the inability to:

- Apply the basic phonics rules in reading
- Write complete sentences
- Automatically read high-frequency words
- Solve simple story problems in math
- Write legibly in cursive (script)

If your third grader is having trouble mastering the above skills, it may be time to schedule a conference with the rest of your child's educational team. This team should include at least you and the primary teacher. Others who may be included on this team may be the school principal, guidance counselor, and/or any other teachers involved with your child this year. More about Parent-Teacher conferences are addressed in Chapter 5.

Should you worry about all of these things? Should that voice be crying out so loud? Yes! You should be concerned; after all, that is what we parents do best. We worry about our little ones as they grow into bigger little ones. Each new step for them sets off warning lights and signal bells within our deepest beings, even if we logically know that everything is ok. Worry is not a bad thing. Concern is not a bad thing. Concern, dealt with in a healthy manner, is what most often leads us to take action and educate ourselves about subjects that we may have been passive about had those worry weeds not taken root. That is what steers us to this book.

THE CHILD

Your Third Grader Is a Unique Child

THERE are many ways to educate a child. Some children attend public school. Others are enrolled in a private or parochial school, and a growing number of families are choosing the path of home schooling. All of these children, though submersed in differing educational environments, share a special set of commonalities. All children are unique in their talents, gifts, and abilities, but all are also very similar in their social and intellectual growth. The third-grade class clown, the third-grade bully, and the third-grade wallflower share many of the same traits, although they do not display them in the same way. Your interest in this book shows that you are interested in learning what the average third grader's abilities, capabilities, and unique needs are, and how you can tailor your child's educational experience to fit your child's nuances.

Some experts claim that a child begins to learn even before birth, while still tucked safely in his mother's womb. We have all watched with wonder as baby talk turns to single-syllable words, then to simple sentences. This is all a very important part of the learning process. Now that your child is preparing to enter third grade, you may feel as though there is a lot that you don't know, when in reality you are already your child's best teacher. While many parents feel powerless when their children head out the door, that feeling is often an inaccurate assessment of your role in your child's education. In many cases, your attitude, involvement, and enthusiasm will set the tone for your child's educational success.

That said, we should define the phrase, "educational success." Educational success does not necessarily mandate that your son or daughter must maintain an "A" average in all subjects. Educational success does not mean that your child's name will be found regularly on the honor roll. Educational success does not mean that your child will win popularity contests. Educational success *does* mean that you, your child, and the teacher(s) assigned to your child will work together to provide the best overall experience for your child, keeping his individual needs in mind, working toward goals, and maintaining a positive attitude toward education.

BUILDING BLOCKS

TO ensure educational success, we first need to understand what our children will be learning in third grade. The learning process in third grade is not unlike the process that your child has experienced his entire life. Just as the baby learns to say a simple sentence by starting with a simple word, your third grader has been learning to succeed since his first day of kindergarten, and even before. The third grade curriculum is a culmination of everything that your child has absorbed in preschool, kindergarten, first, and second grade. Your awareness of the third grade expectations will enhance your third grader's chances of achieving educational success.

Your child will be "reading to learn" instead of "learning to read." Reading is the centerpiece of the third grade year. Much of this year's learning will be dependent on your child's reading and comprehension skills. Even in math class, reading surfaces in the form of word problems. Expect your child to learn more about the world around him in Science and Social Studies. Many third graders are very excited about all of the new facts they are learning and will want to share this new knowledge with you.

SOME HIGHLIGHTS OF LEARNING

THERE is a lot of learning to be done this year. You can measure your child's progress by checking off each of the following skills as they are mastered. Remember, these are only guidelines. Your third grader may be a more advanced or a little behind these general guidelines.

> ➤ The ability to pronounce unfamiliar words
> ➤ The ability to comprehend what they have read
> ➤ Use the dictionary
> ➤ Recognize simple subjects and predicates (nouns and verbs)
> ➤ Write sentences with noun/verb agreement

➤ Write paragraphs with a topic/main idea sentence and supporting details
➤ Add and subtract any numbers 100 – 1,000
➤ Multiplication tables from 1 x 1 = 1 to 9 x 9 = 81 and be able to determine each related division fact
➤ Measure using standard and metric units

SOCIAL BUTTERFLY

ALTHOUGH Chapter 4 of this book delves into social and emotional growth of the third grader, it is important for us to mention now that third grade is a year of social explosion. Your third grader's personality is beginning to grow and shine. Whereas previously this personality was reserved for the safe confines of home or grandma's house, your third grader is now anxious to shine at school as well. These emotional and social changes may cause growing pains for your child, and for you. Rest assured that this is the beginning of your third grader discovering her individuality.

Cliques form within the classroom now, especially among girls. You may find that the best friend status is attached to only one classmate, rather than the revolving door of new best friends announced every other day that you became accustomed to in second grade. Of course this sudden attachment to a schoolmate could lead to a few tears at home. Feelings can and will get hurt while the classroom pecking order sorts itself out. These hurt feelings and small spats usually work themselves out within a day or so without parental intervention.

Clothes, school supplies, and toys take on a new meaning now as your third grader begins to become aware of social status and peer pressure begins to take life. Fads such as Pokémon and Beanie Babies, take hold with a vengeance. There are many lessons to be learned this year, not just academically, but also socially.

The third-grade child is also very inquisitive at home. He will enjoy discussion, and he is beginning to learn how to think through a problem. This year often introduces opportunities for parents to discuss why something is "right" or "wrong." The precocious third grader will often refuse to accept things at face value and will challenge both parents and teachers by asking, "Why?"

As important as you are to your third grader, you may find that when in the company of his friends, your displays of affection are rebuked. Whereas he previously would walk hand in hand with you at a school event, he will now want to walk independently enjoying only your close proximity to give him security. The third grader takes a lot of pride in his parents, but public displays of affection may be met with wincing and eye rolling. Initially shocked, and probably a bit hurt, you will look at your growing child with pride as he becomes more and more comfortable with his newly discovered independence.

"Parents and families are the first and most important teachers. If families teach a love of learning, it can make all the difference in the world to our children."

—RICHARD W. RILEY, U.S. SECRETARY OF EDUCATION

THE PARENT
Where Do I Fit in?

ACCORDING to the National Parent Teacher Association (PTA), "Research shows that when parents are involved in students' education, those students generally have higher grades and test scores, better attendance, and more consistently completed homework." Children who see their parents—and this term can encompass grandparents, guardians, caretakers, relatives—take an active interest in their education tend to view school more seriously and with more respect. Parental involvement is a wonderful, rewarding, and important way to be a good role model to your third grader.

What exactly is the term "parental involvement?" You may have wondered exactly what that phrase means. Do you remember beating yourself up because you were unable to be a classroom volunteer, or to attend the Parent-Teacher-Student Organization (PTSO) meeting at your public school? Let's take the time to reflect on the different parent involvement styles. There are some parents who become involved in their child's education by becoming members of the school board. Others devote time to the PTA, the PTSO, and the Parent-Teacher Organization (PTO). Still a different group of parents are classroom volunteers who assist teachers with day-to-day tasks in the classroom. Many times the least recognized of the involved parents are those who, within the confines of their own homes, spend time with, listen to, create plans for, and learn about their children. You may find that you fall under several of the following categories; which parent involvement style(s) fit you?

Political

The politically involved parent often runs for a seat on the local school board. This parent will assist in making decisions that affect the student body and community as a whole. Budgetary needs are outlined, school policies are created and ratified, and personnel issues are dealt with by the politically involved parent. If not seated on the school board, this parent may find other political avenues to affect the local public school system. This could include running for community government seats, or lobbying those who are in power. This parent writes letters to the editor, attends school board meetings, and is often the author of petitions.

Organizational

Similar to the politically involved parent, the organizationally involved parent is part of an established group of decisionmakers. These parents are members or officers in the PTA, PTO, PTSO, or Parent's Club at their child's school. Meant to be a voice for parents, these organizations promote open communication between the entire educational team. They often sponsor fund-raising events to provide supplies, technology, or educational tools to the school. These groups of organizationally involved parents fund many student field trips.

Volunteers/Aides

The volunteer parent spends time at school, school events, or other volunteer positions. This parent can also be found coaching children's sports, teaching Sunday School, or leading a den of Cub Scouts or Brownies. This parent will be seen sitting at the back of the classroom organizing worksheets for tomorrow's lessons, or in the library shelving books. With school budgets being decimated, and community programs being downgraded, the volunteer is becoming more important than ever. This is why you will see parent volunteers chaperoning fundraising events, manning the bake sale, or providing refreshments at a civic event. The volunteer parental involvement style is often entered into by accident. Your inquisitiveness about your child's school life leads you to attend special functions, and "since you are going anyway . . . " becomes a wonderful excuse to lend a helping hand. You coach softball because your daughter is playing on the team, or become a den parent for your son's Cub Scout den. Remember that being a volunteer is not only helpful to your school or civic organization, but you are also providing your children with a wonderful example of community service.

Private

Although this is the only parental involvement style that does not put the parent in the public eye, it is extremely important. The privately involved parent spends time listening to their child, assisting with homework, and educating themselves to better help their child succeed. Not a day goes by where this parent does not have at least one thought of teaching their child through a life lesson. This parent lives within each of us; we only need to know how to tap into that person to become the best privately involved parent possible. Your interest in this book automatically qualifies you for this parental involvement style!

Most of us will find that we fill no less than one of the above involvement styles, but we may fit all four. It is imperative that as a parent we understand our talents and personalities to know how to best be involved in our children's educational experience. Not all parents are cut out to fit all of the roles above, while others may balance them easily.

Education is too important to be left solely to the educators.

—FRANCIS KEPPEL, FORMER U.S. COMMISSIONER OF EDUCATION

WHY SHOULD I GET INVOLVED?

I WON'T ever forget my first formal parental involvement experience. My oldest was in kindergarten. Yearning to share with him, I chose a day and time that fit my schedule to volunteer in the classroom. There I sat, in the back of the room, knees tucked under a very small table, seated in an even smaller chair. Before me was a large pile of Campbell's Soup labels. Some were in plastic grocery bags, others rolled into tight wads secured by rubber bands, and the remainder piled, not unlike fall leaves, into a heap. The task before me was to unwrap the labels and rewrap them in quantities of twenty-five. Easy enough, right?

I counted, wrapped, counted wrapped, all the while observing the classroom dynamics. One ear was honing in on the veteran teacher, who was enchanting the children with a story about Mr. H, who wore a hat. The scratchy tones of an old record player soon filled the room as the children heard a song all about Mr. H. While entranced in the Mr. H song, worksheets appeared, as if by magic, on the children's tables. Twenty-three, twenty-four, twenty-five, now wrap. Giggles and conversation ensued as the children completed their worksheets about the happy Mr. H. During recess the children could be heard on the playground singing the song about Mr. H.

That day my son learned about the letter H, but I learned so much more. I had a brief window on his world. I got to know the teacher a bit better, recognized the children by name, and became acclimated to the rules and structure within the school. All of this information served me well. When it came time for parent-teacher conference, I did not find the teacher as intimidating as I might have otherwise. When my son talked about Justin or Philip, I knew whom he meant and could engage him in more conversation. Lastly, I felt comfortable walking into the school, talking to the educational staff, and dealing with any questions that arose.

Being involved in your child's education has its rewards. Not only are you on the path to being the parent of a successful adult, you are educating yourself. You are your child's best advocate, and your best tool as an advocate is knowledge. Not every parent is able to volunteer at school, and no one should feel like a failure for not doing so, but every parent should take the time to get to know their child's teacher, who their child's classmates are, the key administrators, and to understand the school policies. Now that my children are older, my main form of parental involvement is private. We spend a lot of time at our home learning, although I am still keeping that a secret from my kids.

SELF-DOUBT AND NEGATIVITY

IF you find that you are reluctant to become involved in your child's educational growth, you may want to ask yourself why. Perhaps your elementary school career was unhappy, or a particular subject always caused you trouble. Come to grips with your own school-related apprehensions. As parents we are in a very powerful position. Our experiences in our elementary education help us ensure that our children's experiences are positive. For example, if dyslexia was an obstacle that you had to work to overcome, you will be better prepared to identify and assist one of your children if he faces a similar difficulty.

The introverted parent may not feel comfortable attending her first PTA meeting, but that same parent may thrive shelving books in the library. Understand that the involved parent does not have to "do it all." Today's culture may lead us to believe that if we are not juggling twenty things at once, we are a failure, but do not allow those pressures to permeate this facet of your life. Recognize your abilities, interests, and capabilities, as well as the logistics of the commitment you are about to make. Be realistic about your commitment. Understand that the school librarian does not expect you to shelve books every day any more than you can make that sort of commitment. If in fact you are able to shelve books every day, rest assured that there are librarians all across the nation who would love to have you join them.

It is imperative not to broadcast a negative attitude toward school or education. A child who is witness to negative behavior or discussion about school from a parent will become negative herself. A parent, who complains about homework openly to his child, will become a parent of a child who views homework with skepticism and a casual disinterest. We are all familiar with the slogan, "You are what you eat." In this case your child "is what you teach."

THE TEACHER
Your Partner in Education

IN third grade your child may have a single teacher throughout the day, or he may visit with several different teachers. One teacher often teaches core subjects, while music, art, foreign language, computer, and physical education are taught by teachers specialized in those disciplines. Each of these educators play an important role in your child's success.

In the previous grades, your child may have had a teacher who was very soft and mothering. It would not be unusual to see the kindergarten, first-, or second-grade teacher tying shoes, zipping coats, and helping the more shy child interact with the group. Each year this kind of interaction wanes as a child's ability grows. By the time your child is promoted to third grade, he will be expected to bear more of his own responsibility. He will be expected to dress himself, be a bit more comfortable in social situations, and responsible for his assignments.

Because the third-grade teacher is probably the first teacher who is perceived more as a teacher and less as a nurturing figure, she or he may be labeled as "mean" or "indifferent" by parents and students. In most cases this could not be farther from the truth. Educators are given the weighty responsibility of ensuring that our children grow into healthy, productive, and happy adults. If your third-grade teacher seems to be expecting a bit more from your third grader, take the time to evaluate her reasons. Might she really be teaching your child to persevere?

It is important that your child is not taught to fear their teacher. The third grader should respect her teacher, and feel comfortable asking questions and joining discussions. Although there may be times when your third grader seems to be angry or upset with her teacher, overall she should feel comfortable around her. Your child's teacher is a critical partner in your child's educational success.

A national study of first through fourth-grade teachers showed that they are spending an average of 11.6 hours a week on activities outside of teaching. Those activities included tutoring, staff meetings, and parent-teacher conferences. Although the teacher's schedule will sometimes dictate a demanding pace, it is important to know that educators enjoy parental involvement and will, in most cases, be eager to answer any questions you may have pertaining to your child's curriculum, social skills, or behavior. Many of the teachers who were contacted during the writing of this book expressed that, because a third-grade child is more independent and exudes a more grown-up air, parental involvement often drops drastically at the third-grade level. This is a trend that all would like to see turned around.

THE EDUCATIONAL TEAM

REMEMBER that the educational team consists of three distinct players: the parent, the teacher, and the child. There are no bench-warmers in this game. All of the players are expected to step up to the plate and give it their best shot. Along the way there could be a few stumbling points—rain delays, so to speak. Perhaps there will even be a period of time where your team seems to be in a slump. All of these are natural events in the learning cycle. As long as you are well prepared, have a good attitude, and are a willing participant in your child's education, everyone wins. We will discuss this team in more depth in Chapter 5 of this book.

Now that we have described the members of the team, and we have given you a rough view of the playing field and conditions, we should jump in and start learning.

OWNER'S MANUAL

CHILDREN are born naked, and unfortunately, as many parents before us have lamented, they do not arrive with an owner's manual in their cute little fisted hands. We understand that the infant must be swaddled for warmth. Our instincts remind us that the little being in our arms must be nourished. Because education is a relatively new offering to the human experience, we do not possess the instinctual ability to just "know" what to expect as that tiny baby grows into the energetic, school-age child. Many help manuals have been written to assist parents with everything from diaper changing to finding money for college. Consider this book your manual to the third-grade experience. It has been compiled with information gleaned from educators, statistics, and most importantly, from other parents just like you and me. Use this book like you use the automobile owner's manual found in your minivan's glove box. Read over it to prepare yourself, and then refer to it often as the third-grade year goes on. Facts, thoughts, and ideas that may seem irrelevant during your first read-through will take on new meaning halfway through the school year when your third grader is struggling with homework, social interactions, or learning a new skill.

What Your Child Is Learning in School

KNOWING what your child is learning in school allows you to be prepared for the questions that your precocious third grader will ask of you. Children of this age usually are very conversational and will enjoy sharing their daily experiences with you. Being prepared allows you to further engage the child in conversation, thus encouraging the child to explore the limits of his mind. Also, having a clear idea of what the third-grade curriculum expectations are will enable you to provide the proper books, software, and activities to expand your third grader's growing intellect.

NO REALLY, WHAT IS MY CHILD LEARNING?

YOU have probably heard stories from parents of children who have already been through the third-grade experience. You may hear comments like, "Oh, it was a very difficult year." or "We had a lot more homework." Other parents may express, "What a wonderful year. Sarah really blossomed."

and "James really matured and learned a lot this year." Third grade may very well rival kindergarten as being the most definitive year in your child's elementary education.

This year will be very different for you and your third grader. There is a new sense of responsibility associated with the learning process. There will be thicker textbooks, heavier backpacks, more stringent homework assignments, and less "play-learning." Perhaps this year will be the first year your child participates in standardized testing.

You will find that the third-grade year is heavy on Reading/Language Arts skills which include Reading, Writing, Spelling, Grammar, and Vocabulary. By the end of this year your already verbose third grader will also be putting her thoughts down into words in he form of reports, short stories, and poetry.

HOW IS THEIR TIME SPENT?

YOUR third grader will be a very busy bee this school year. She will head off to school in the morning, with the previous evening's homework assignments completed, ready for another full day of learning. Although every school has it's own schedule, a typical third grader's daily schedule may look like the sample below.

THIRD GRADE CLASS SCHEDULE

8:45–9:15	Opening and Board Work
9:15–10:00	Reading/Language Arts
10:00–10:20	Break
10:20–11:15	Mathematics
11:15–12:00	Rotating Subjects
12:00–12:30	Lunch
12:30–1:45	Writing Workshop
1:45–2:00	Independent Work (silent reading or journal writing)
2:00–2:30	Recess
2:30–3:30	Social Studies and Science
3:35	Dismissal

ROTATING SUBJECTS (11:15–12:00)

Monday:	Foreign Language
Tuesday:	Music
Wednesday:	Computer
Thursday:	Art
Friday:	Physical Education

As the schedule shows, throughout the day, your third grader will be taking part in activities and lessons covering a wide variety of topics. According to a report commissioned by the United States Department of Education, your child will spend an average of almost six and a half hours per day learning at school. This figure does not include activities such as recess and lunch, which provide their own unique social learning opportunities. Of those six and a half hours each day, approximately four hours a day are spent covering the core subjects, Reading, Mathematics, Science, and Social Studies. Those four hours can be further broken down to include:

➤ 2 hours a day (50%) spent on Reading/Language Arts
➤ 1 hour a day (24%) spent working with Mathematics
➤ 35 minutes a day (13%) devoted to Science
➤ 35 minutes a day (13%) devoted to Social Studies

The remaining two and a half hours a day are spent on some of the Arts/Athletics classes, morning announcements, enrichment activities, transitional time (the time spent putting books away and retrieving text books for the next lesson), and preparation time (preparing for lunch, preparing for afternoon dismissal, etc.).

Surprisingly these numbers are very similar nationwide. There are small variances from state to state, but those variances are minimal. There are also negligible variances between public and private schools. This observation shows us that although teaching strategies may differ, the amount of time spent instructing our children in the core curriculum subjects remains constant.

You can find information about your state's standards with just the click of a mouse. Go to www.eduhound.com and click on "Standards by State." You can easily find information about what your state expects of your child. If you would like to find more information about your school or other schools, you can use the American School Directory at www.asd.com to find everything from cafeteria menus to class size.

Learning the Language of Education

As parents, we often struggle with the learning curve ourselves. While school administrators and educators may outline the third-grade curriculum, it is often done in verbiage unfamiliar to those outside of the education profession. For instance, you may have heard the terms "whole language" and "phonics" but do you really know what they mean? By the time you finish reading this chapter you will have a better understanding of those terms, and many others.

Although every school has it's own curriculum, the basic third grade includes Reading and Language Arts, Writing, Math, Science, and Social Studies. Also included in the typical third grade are music, computer, art, physical education, and foreign language classes.

Let's try to explain the curriculum associated with each of the above in lay terms.

I loved teaching in third-grade classrooms. The students learn so much in that grade, and they take that knowledge with them for the rest of their lives. It's the BEST year for kids in school. They get much—cursive writing, the REAL math stuff—multiplication and division—they learn how to USE numbers and make them work for them. They read chapter books and struggle with reading aloud—trying to sound so big. Can you tell that I loved it?

—A FORMER TUTOR FROM INDIANA

CORE SUBJECTS

Reading

READING, the first of the infamous "Three R's" takes center stage in third grade. Children are now "reading to learn" instead of "learning to read."

Academically, your son or daughter should have a grasp of basic reading skills. During the previous primary grades, the typical child has begun reading easy-to-read books. By third grade, your child may be reading young reader chapter books. While reading aloud is still very important, the third grader is expected to also stay focused during silent reading.

The ability to comprehend, or understand, what is read is key in third grade, when more lessons are taught using textbooks and written teaching materials. Reading permeates every one of your child's classes this year, including math. If your third grader is experiencing difficulty reading, it will become more obvious this year, and remedial classes may be introduced at this time. If your child is a prolific reader, and understands what she has read, she will have a head start to learning in the other subjects covered this year.

Students in third grade will ingest fictional and non-fictional works geared toward honing reading comprehension skills. Instead of stories concluding with a straightforward message, students are encouraged to think about what they have read, investigate personalities or facts presented, and discuss the less obvious themes hidden within the text.

Your child will also be expected to surmise if a story is real or make-believe. This is often done by way of studying the difference between "tall tales" and folk stories, and historical events. An example would be discussing the difference between the story of George Washington chopping down the cherry tree versus the story of George Washington crossing the Delaware. While both stories include a historical figure, one story is more clearly based on fact.

According to the National Reading Panel, in order for children to be good readers, they must be taught:

- phonemic awareness skills: the ability to manipulate the sounds that make up spoken language
- phonics skills: the understanding that there are relationships between letters and sounds
- the ability to read fluently with accuracy, speed, and expression
- to apply reading comprehension strategies to enhance understanding and enjoyment of what they read

For more information about the National Reading Panel, and their reports, visit their website at www.nationalreadingpanel.org.

A sample curriculum outline could read as below:

➤ READING UNFAMILIAR MATERIAL

- Sounding out words phonetically
- Recognizing words based on familiar words in context
- Skip, read-on, re-read
- Use prior knowledge to recognize a word

This module is building upon the basic concepts taught since the beginning of your child's education. Your child will be encouraged to use a variety of tactics to correctly read an unknown word or phrase. Note that both phonics and whole language are encouraged in this module. Please read on to learn more about these language acquisition methods and how they intersect.

➤ READING COMPREHENSION

- Use context clues
- Re-reading of an item for analysis
- Reading aloud
- Use illustrations, diagrams maps, and charts surrounding the written piece to gain understanding
- Use prior knowledge

As mentioned above, comprehension is extremely important this year. Your child will need to sharpen his comprehension skills in order to succeed in all subjects. The National Institute of Child Health and Human Development suggests, "comprehension of text is best facilitated by teaching students a variety of techniques and systematic strategies to assist in recall of information, question generation, and summarizing of information."

➤ UNDERSTANDING SENTENCE/PARAGRAPH STRUCTURE

- Main idea
- Details
- Chronological order and event sequencing
- Problem/Solution

- Characterization
- Cause and effect

Basic sentence and paragraph structure is introduced to children. After reading a paragraph, your third grader may be asked "Which sentence contains the main idea of this paragraph?" The ability to understand events, how they relate to one another, and in what logical order they should be placed will be practiced this year.

➤ ANALYZING

- Make and verify predictions
- Discuss problems and solutions
- Draw conclusions, evaluate solutions, and recognize feelings and motives

The third-grade problem solver shines while analyzing events, predicting outcomes of stories, and working with classmates to assemble solutions. She may be asked how the main character of a story could have behaved differently to change the outcome of a story.

➤ RELATING

- Ask, "How does this affect me?"

Children may be asked, after reading a selection, "How does this story affect you?" "Have you ever found yourself in a similar situation?" This gives new importance to reading. A child will now read a selection because they enjoy that the hero in the story is the same age as they are, or because they also have a little sister.

➤ READING APPRECIATION

- Reading for fun
- Participate in improvisations, play reading
- Reading voluntarily for information

The third-grade reading list will include a variety of selections. Some will be fiction, others fact. Some of the selections will be serious, and perhaps a bit difficult for even the most advanced third-grade reader. Other selections will be fun and playful, engaging the entire class. Special reading incentive programs such as "Book It!" or Accelerated Reader may be introduced this year to help encourage casual reading. Be sure to look into some of the recommendations made by other parents and teachers in the Resources section at the end of this book.

➤ LITERATURE

During this school year, your child's reading preferences may change as he is exposed to a wide array of literature. He will be encouraged to read full-length juvenile novels, poetry, plays, fables, and nonfiction. He may begin to understand poetry, take an interest in the classics, or begin to choose books to read by a favorite author. Some books that have proved to be perennial favorites include the Ramona series by Beverly Cleary, as well as the Little House on the Prairie series, by Laura Ingalls Wilder. Of course, there is always room for new classics such as the Harry Potter series.

THE PHONICS VERSUS WHOLE LANGUAGE DEBATE

MOST parents have heard the terms, "phonics" and "whole language" used in conversations about their child's reading curriculum. Although many of us may feel pressured to take a stand on this issue, it is important that we understand both terms, how they fit with our child's learning style, and how we can use the best features of each teaching style to ensure our child's success.

Phonics

Many parents feel comfortable with this teaching style because it is probably the way we were taught to read. Remember sitting at your little desk sounding out words on the blackboard, "b . . . at, b . . . at, bat? bat. Bat!" There is a certain level of comfort in teaching our children with the same instructional methods used by our teachers. A child with a more structured, regimental learning style will usually succeed with this teaching method.

Whole Language

The whole language approach to reading encourages children to learn to read in the same method that they learned to speak. Children learn to speak by observing the world around them, and gradual memorization of attaching words to objects or feelings. This is also true for whole language. The child learns to read by looking at a language as a whole, and gradually learning words as they gain importance to him. A child who is a more hands-on, tactile learner will usually succeed with this teaching method.

A Mixture of the Two

Many parents and teachers are now finding that a good mixture of phonics *and* whole language is necessary to provide the best reading foundation for our children. Because different children have different learning styles, a combination of teaching strategies will engage more children in the classroom, promote a greater understanding of written material, and therefore create the foundation for success.

The National Association for the Education of Young Children suggests that phonics and whole language be combined. "Phonics should not be taught as a separate 'subject' with

When it comes to reading, or any subject for that matter, understanding your child's learning style is crucial. You may notice that your child learns best when he is instructed verbally, or you may notice that he won't understand something, unless he sees it. Here is a breakdown of the four learning styles that will help you provide him with the teaching strategy that is the closest match.

THE FOUR WAYS IN WHICH CHILDREN LEARN

- **Tactile Learning.** Children who are tactile learners learn best when they can touch and manipulate things. If these children come into physical contact with the material at hand—that is, if they can handle it, take it apart and put it together—they do their best learning.
- **Visual Learning.** These children learn best when they see things. For them, seeing leads to understanding. Tell a visual learner something, and she will forget it. Let her see it, and the chances are good that it's cemented in her brain.
- **Auditory Learning.** Auditory learners are those children who learn most effectively when they hear the material. Verbal instructions are a breeze. These children like to have new ideas explained to them rather than shown to them. They are good listeners.
- **Kinesthetic Learning.** Children who need to have some kind of active experience with something to best process new information are called kinesthetic learners. Action, movement, motion, and rhythm—even dancing and singing—will enhance a learning situation for these children.

—From *A Parent's Guide to 2nd Grade*, by Peter W. Cookson, Jr., Ph.D. and Marion Hess Pomeranc, M.S.

emphasis on drills and rote memorization. The key is a balanced approach and attention to each child's individual needs. Many children's understanding of phonics will arise from their interest, knowledge, and ideas. Others will benefit from more formal instruction. There are many opportunities to teach the sound a letter makes when children have reason to know. For example, the first letter a child learns typically is the first letter of her name."

Also supporting the mixed approach to learning is Education Secretary Richard W. Riley. Responding to a March 18, 1998 report entitled, "Preventing Reading Difficulties in Young Children," Riley said, "The study clearly defines the key elements all children need in order to become good readers. Specifically, kids need to learn letters and sounds and how to read for meaning. They also need opportunities to practice reading with many types of books. While some children need more intensive and systematic individualized instruction than others, all children need these three essential elements in order to read well and independently by the end of third grade. Effective teaching and extra resources can make it possible for many 'at-risk' children to become successful leaders."

LANGUAGE ARTS

NOW that we have discussed how our children are learning to read, the next step is to discuss how they are learning to use the English language to convey their own original ideas and thoughts. Language Arts includes spelling, sentence structure, and writing—both handwriting and the actual creation of a written piece aimed at a particular audience.

The third-grade year is all about communication and sharing, hence the emphasis on Reading and Language Arts. Good Reading and Language Arts skills are important across the entire third-grade curriculum as your child is expected to communicate thoughts and solutions in a more organized manner.

Language Arts encompasses vocabulary, spelling, and both written and spoken language. Your child's curriculum may include any or all of the following:

➤ READ AND WRITE LETTER-SOUND COMBINATIONS

Your third grader should be very familiar with the letter-sound combinations such as those in the list below.

wh	fr	pl	sc	sm
th	cr	sl	st	sw
ch	tr	gl	sp	shr
sh	dr	bl	sn	spr
kn	br	fl	squ	
wr	pr	cl	scr	
gr	thr	sk	str	

➤ ABILITY TO CREATE A SYNOPSIS

The ability to comprehend what is read is often evaluated by a child's ability to then explain, in a nutshell, the paragraph, selection, or book. Book reports or "How I spent my summer vacation" writing assignments are examples of the creation of a synopsis.

➤ CHECK WORK

Understand and practice proofreading skills such as how to check for correct grammar, capitalization, punctuation, spelling as well as handwriting accuracy.

➤ THIRD-GRADE VOCABULARY

Vocabulary and spelling go hand in hand. Vocabulary stresses the meanings and correct uses of words, whereas spelling stresses the correct spelling of words.

➤ PROFICIENT SPELLING

The one topic that I hear about repeatedly among parents of third graders is spelling. Because the third grader usually brings home a new list of spelling words each week, this is the one subject where the parent is usually most involved. Your child's teacher may follow a schedule similar to the one below for the weekly spelling unit:

Monday: Introduce new words
Tuesday: Take pretest plus spelling homework is assigned
Wednesday: Review spelling words plus spelling homework is assigned
Thursday: Take second pretest
Friday: Weekly spelling test

In addition to regular spelling lists, your third grader may be expected to spell commonly used words such as number words to 100, days of the week, and months of the year. Either within the spelling or language arts classes, your child will also learn to capitalize appropriate holidays, titles, countries, and titles of respect (such as Mr. and Mrs.).

Sample Spelling Lists:

about	far
again	farther
always	farthest
another	dirtier
around	easier
because	funniest
could	grumpier
enough	grumpy
every	higher
found	fastest

Grammar

There is a lot to be learned grammatically this year as well. This year your third grader will learn to:

➤ IDENTIFY AND USE COMPOUND WORDS

Your child's growing vocabulary will include larger, multi-syllable words. Some of these words will be compound words. Not only will your child be encouraged to read compound words, but he will be expected to dissect a compound word into its two simple word parts. Examples of third-grade-level compound words are:

paintbrush	sandbox	bathtub
afternoon	sunshine	farmhouse

➤ ALPHABETIZATION

Your child is now learning that order and sequencing is important to organizing everyday life. Along with chronology taught in Language Arts, he will learn to put up to five words in alphabetical order by at least the first and second letter. Your third grader should be able to alphabetize the following list of words:

mime
nature
love
nickel
monkey

➤ UTILIZE RESOURCE MATERIALS APPROPRIATELY

During this year, your third grader will begin to utilize resource materials such as dictionaries, encyclopedias, or the world atlas.

➤ SHARE THOUGHTS VERBALLY

Your child may be asked to do his first oral report this year. In addition, he will be expected to answer questions in all subjects clearly.

➤ SHARE THOUGHTS IN WRITTEN FORMAT

Along with sharing verbally, your third grader will be asked to write down thoughts, research, or solutions in written format.

➤ USE CORRECT PUNCTUATION

Children will learn the correct use of commas, periods, question marks, apostrophes, and exclamation points.

➤ COMPLETE A RESEARCH PROJECT USING SEVERAL RESOURCES

Tying your child's newly discovered writing and research skills together will be at least one research project. This project may be completed independently, or perhaps a team of third graders will work together to complete it.

➤ CORRECTLY ABBREVIATE DAYS OF WEEK, MONTHS, ADDRESS WORDS, TIME

Sunday	Sun.
Monday	Mon.
Tuesday	Tues. (Tue.)
Wednesday	Wed.
Thursday	Thurs. (Thu.)
Friday	Fri.
Saturday	Sat.
January	Jan.
February	Feb.
March	Mar.
April	Apr.
May	May
June	June (Jun.)
July	July (Jul.)
August	Aug.
September	Sept. (Sep.)
October	Oct.
November	Nov.

December	Dec.
Street	St.
Avenue	Ave.
Post Office Box	P.O. Box
Second	sec.
Minute	min.
Hour	hr. (h.)
Before Noon	A.M.
After Noon	P.M.

➤ IDENTIFY PARTS OF ENGLISH

The English language is made up of several parts of speech. This year your third grader will learn more about those parts of speech and how they fit together.

Nouns—a type of word that gives a name to a person, place, or thing.
Verbs—a type of word that suggests an action.
Adjectives—a type of word that describes a noun.
Adverbs—a type of word that describes a verb (usually ends with the -ly suffix).

➤ SPEAK AND WRITE WITH TENSE AGREEMENT

There will be an added emphasis on using correct grammar in both written and spoken language. Your third grader will learn to use correct subject–verb agreement.

Incorrect:　　The dogs in the yard is barking.
Correct:　　The dogs in the yard are barking.

➤ SPEAK AND WRITE WITH APPROPRIATE WORD ORDER

Understand and use correct sentence structure. Your third grader should have a thorough understanding that all complete sentences must contain a noun and a verb. He should also be able to speak and write using correct sentence structure, using adverbs and adjectives to completely describe thoughts and to accurately convey the desired message.

"The limits of your language are the limits of your world."

—LUDWIG WITTGENSTEIN, AUTHOR, TEACHER, AND PHILOSOPHER

Writing

The goals of a Language Arts curriculum state that not only should a child understand the English language, they should also be able to communicate effectively using it. Third-grade students are expected to communicate their thoughts using written language. Your child will

➤ Write thank you notes, greeting cards, friendly letters, and invitations
➤ Write formula poetry such as haiku and limerick
➤ Compose well-thought and well-written answers to essay questions
➤ Use writing as a tool for learning and thinking across the curriculum

There is a continued emphasis on the writing process. Your third grader will compose many works this year, including research articles and short stories.

GREAT IDEA!

One mother mused, "One of the most cherished keepsakes I have from my sons' elementary years is a stack of journals." Indeed, there is nothing like looking back at how they used to be. Encourage your child to keep a journal of his thoughts, ideas, feelings, daily routines, and even drawings. Not only will it give him the opportunity to practice writing, but it will give you both a chance to enjoy memories of his early years long after he is grown.

Cursive Writing

While, at the beginning of the third-grade year, your child may only be expected to print with care, utilizing margin and indentation, cursive writing is just around the corner. Throughout your third grader's short school career, he has been printing. Cursive writing is usually introduced in third grade. Some children struggle with the eye-hand coordination to create the looping letters, while others will still be struggling to print legibly. Don't worry if writing takes time to master, practice makes perfect.

There are some basic rules that your third grader can practice that will encourage good cursive writing skills.

1. Keep feet flat on the floor
2. Sit comfortably in a chair, bending the entire upper body slightly forward
3. Place both arms on the desk, with elbows off the edge
4. Place paper correctly on the desk, at a slight angle
5. Hold the pencil correctly
6. Use the non-writing hand to move the paper while writing

Expectations for cursive writing in the classroom may be similar to those listed below:

➤ Lower-case cursive letters taught during first nine weeks
➤ Upper-case cursive letters taught during the second nine weeks
➤ Students will be expected to use cursive writing in homework and class work assignments

Arithmetic

By third grade, your child should also have mastered some basic math skills. Basic addition facts are ready to be built upon this year. Subtraction facts have also been practiced repeatedly, and your third grader should be feeling comfortable with basic subtraction. While your child may have been introduced to multiplication in second grade, multiplication and division will be explored in depth this year. Simple geometry skills will be introduced, and more shapes and concepts may be covered during this year. Children in third grade will measure in standard feet and inches as well as converting those measurements to the metric system.

➤ READ, WRITE, COUNT, COMPARE, AND ESTIMATE WHOLE NUMBERS

After becoming familiar with numbers over the past few years, your child is now ready to manipulate them and learn to use them for his own purposes. Analysis of how numbers relate to one another is also built upon. For instance:

$5 < 8$	Five is less than eight
$6 > 3$	Six is greater than three
$5 = 2 + 3$	Five equals two plus three
$5 < 2 + 2$	Five is less than two plus two

➤ RECOGNIZE SIMILARITIES AND PATTERNS IN SETS AND NUMBERS

Your third grader may be expected to complete these types of patterns:

2, 5, 9, 14, __   (The number 20 completes this pattern)

1, 2, 11, __, 111, 222   (The number 22 completes this pattern)

➤ IDENTIFY GEOMETRIC SHAPES

In third grade, your child is expected to know the following geometric shapes:

Circle
Triangle
Square
Rectangle

Pentagon
Hexagon
Octagon

➤ USE NUMBER LINES, CHARTS, MAPS, GRIDS

Understanding mathematical expressions is often best accomplished with visual tools. The third-grade student will learn to use these tools to help him visualize mathematical problems, and arrive at appropriate solutions. Learning to read graphs, such as the one found below allows students, especially visual learners, to read and understand information that isn't written with numerals. This sort of mathematical reasoning will become increasingly relevant as students begin to take standardized tests.

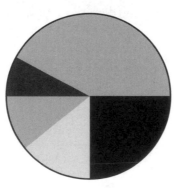

➤ MEASURE TEMPERATURE, TIME, AND SIZE

Learning relativity requires the ability to measure. Children measure almost everything at this age, from temperature, to time.

If your child does not know how to read an analog clock (the kind with hands) by now, he will learn this year. Not only will he learn know how to read an analog clock, he will also gain a better understanding of time. A typical word problem may ask:

It is now 3:15 P.M. John must pick up his little sister, Dawn, from her school in a half hour. At what time does John have to pick up Dawn?

He will also learn to measure common objects using both the metric system and the standard American measuring system. Height, weight, length, width, and depth are all covered this year.

➤ WORK MATHEMATICALLY WITH MONEY

Imagine how important your third grader will feel when he brings home play money and practices adding, subtracting, and figuring with the pretend coins. Children at this age should have experience with counting and adding money. As children become older and earn, spend, and save money, they should be familiar with all denominations of U.S. money.

➤ COLLECT AND ORGANIZE DATA

Your child may perform simple studies in his classroom to illustrate the importance of numbers in every day life. For example, your child may create a survey asking classmates what school lunch is the favorite. Results will then be compiled, perhaps a graph drawn and then your third grader will write a brief one or two sentence synopsis of the study.

➤ ADD AND SUBTRACT USING NUMBERS CONTAINING UP TO FOUR DIGITS

Numerical manipulation continues as your third grader will be performing more complex addition and subtraction problems.

$$
\begin{array}{ccc}
1016 & 243 & 2806 \\
-483 & +699 & +1111 \\
\hline
\end{array}
$$

➤ MULTIPLY AND DIVIDE THROUGH THE "9s"

Now that your third grader has mastered addition and subtraction facts, it is time to learn to multiply and divide. Most multiplication learning is done by way of memorization, repetition, and practice. While some students struggle with multiplication, it is a necessary skill needed for math classes throughout elementary and high school. To help keep their multiplication facts straight, students may be asked to complete worksheet such as the one below. The student should multiply each of the numbers from the top column, with each of the numbers in the row on the left, then write the result in the appropriate square. We have completed one through three for you.

Multiply	1	2	3	4	5	6	7	8	9
1	1	2	3						
2	2	4	6						
3	3	6	9						
4	4	8	12						
5	5	10	15						
6	6	12	18						
7	7	14	21						
8	8	16	24						
9	9	18	27						

➤ BASIC UNDERSTANDING OF FRACTIONS

Using simple illustrations and mental imagery, your third grad-er will obtain a basic understanding of fractional values (½, ¼, ⅓, ⅛). Fractions can be a difficult concept to many budding mathe-maticians. Visual examples help children to grasp the idea of parts of a whole. As math problems become more complex, including multiplying and subtracting fractions, children will need to rely on a strong familiarity and comfort with fractions.

1/5   3/4   1/4   4/5

Social Studies

Until now, your third grader probably has had a very limited perception of the world around him. His "world" includes first and foremost, himself, followed by his parents, siblings, and close family and friends. This year he will come to understand that *his* world is only a small part of a much larger community—town, state, country, and world.

During the third grade, civics and government are often covered, as well as major events in history. Your third grader will be introduced to a growing cast of people important in history. For the first time your third grader may understand the Revolutionary War, or Martin Luther King, Jr. Day. Suddenly he will become aware of the world around him, and the events that helped to shape it.

Possible concepts taught in third grade Social Studies could include:

➤ RECOGNIZE PEOPLE AS MEMBERS OF COMMUNITIES

The study of people, small communities, cities, counties, states, and countries creates the framework necessary for your child to understand basic concepts of how the world around him works.

➤ IDENTIFY MAPS, GLOBES, TIME LINES, CHARTS, GRAPHS

Your third grader's classroom will probably have at least one globe, several maps, and perhaps a few other charts. Until now, your child may have only seen these items as decoration for the classroom. This year he will learn the functionality of maps and globes as he learns about community, countries, and the fundamentals of distance. Be prepared for him to use words such as longitude and latitude when describing his daily lessons.

➤ DEVELOP KNOWLEDGE OF HISTORY AND GEOGRAPHY OF LOCAL COMMUNITY AND COUNTRY

Perhaps a complete unit in social studies will be devoted to your child's immediate community. He will learn when his community was settled, who the prominent citizens were, and what types of industry were common in the community's infancy.

➤ BECOME AWARE OF BEING A PATRIOTIC CITIZEN

The Pledge of Allegiance takes on new importance to the third grader. He will begin to understand, albeit on a very basic level, the meaning of patriotism and loyalty to country. He will suddenly have an awareness that there are many other countries in his world, when up until now, he may not have realized there were any.

Some of the types of social studies questions your child may encounter may be as follows:

What is the capital of France?
A. London
B. Paris
C. Ireland
D. Great Britain

Which of the following is NOT an ocean:
A. Indian
B. Pacific
C. Atlantic
D. European

Put the following items in the order they were invented:
Car, Computer, Wheel, Telephone

Match the following capitals with their state.

California	Albany
New Mexico	Cheyenne
New York	Santa Fe
Wyoming	Sacramento

➤ BECOME AWARE OF CURRENT EVENTS

For the first time, your third grader may take interest in the newspaper or nightly news program. He will be expected to be able to discuss some current events at school, and how those events may shape tomorrow's world.

Science

There is a growing awareness of the world around us in third grade. In learning about the animals and plants that inhabit the world around us, the third grader will also learn about recycling and reusing. You may find that your child refuses to throw away aluminum cans, and suddenly becomes a willing helper in the weekly recycling chores.

Some sample third-grade science units could include:

➤ SIMPLE MACHINES

Have you ever wondered, "How does a teeter-totter work?" Do you remember asking yourself, "Why do things fall down instead of up?" Many of these types of questions will be answered in third-grade science. In third grade, simple machines are often introduced, as well as basic principles of physics. Children learn about pulleys, levers, and other simple machines.

➤ HABITAT/ADAPTATION

If there is a pond or wetland near your child's school, the class may slip on galoshes and visit it for a day or so. While there, they may collect tadpoles, explore the various types of wildlife found in the area, and note the unique plant-life found in the pond, near the pond and finally, the plant-life in the surrounding meadow, forest, or fields.

➤ FOOD CHAINS

While learning about the food chain, your child will learn the basic "circle of life." Plants are eaten by insects, which are eaten by birds, which are eaten by larger carnivores, which are eventually eaten by even larger carnivores, or by man.

➤ ANIMAL KINGDOM

The third grader will learn about the animals from long ago—such as dinosaurs, as well as species being newly discovered in the rain forests. Terms such as *extinction*, though difficult for many third graders to pronounce, becomes commonplace as endangered species are discussed. Your child may also learn the basic differences between mammals, fish, insects, reptiles, amphibians, and birds.

➤ SOLAR SYSTEM

Don't be surprised if, during a clear night, your third grader points to the heavens and proclaims, "There's Orion!" The solar system is often one of the most popular science units covered in third grade.

Foreign Language

Not all schools offer a foreign language in the elementary years, but if your child's school does, the following may be covered:

➤ Conjugation of basic verbs
➤ Increase vocabulary to include the alphabet, numbers to 100, colors, food, time, and professions
➤ Simple dialogue and conversation including the vocabulary
➤ Folk songs or fairy tales in the foreign language

Arts and Athletics

Music, Library, Art, and Physical Education classes are the norm this year, as they have been for the past two years. Usually your third grader will have one of these special classes a day. Many schools will require that Physical Education classes take place twice a week, while the other classes take place once a week. Most third graders look forward to these special classes sprinkled throughout their week. Another teacher within the school system most commonly teaches these classes. This gives the child a change of pace, change of scenery, and change of teacher in their day.

These special classes also provide enrichment to your child's education. Enrichment can best be described as the broadening of horizons. While your child is learning the basics of education by studying the core curriculum subjects, the special classes expose the third grader to subjects, theories, and arts that may not be readily available at home or in the conventional classroom setting.

Music

Most children of this age enjoy a wide variety of music. Often they can be heard singing, seen dancing, and found tapping their feet and clapping their hands to music. Studies have shown that there is a basic correlation between music and mathematics. Music is historical, mathematical, analytical, scientific, and emotional. A healthy appreciation for many musical styles and types directly influences a child's ability understanding across the curriculum. Also, children who have difficulty learning in a conventional learning environment often thrive when their learning is more arts–based. Music is one of the tools used to reach the arts–based learner. Listening to, understanding, and appreciating music actually encourages academic growth and success. The third-grade musician will learn to:

➤ Recognize different tempos and tempo changes in a variety of musical settings (Tempo is the rhythm and speed of a musical composition.)
➤ Identify stylistic differences in individual styles of music—be able to listen to a musical selection and label it as classical, folk, pop, opera, or rock
➤ Extend skills at note reading
➤ Explore genre of country music through instruments, folk songs, classical music
➤ Extend skills on recorder—a recorder is an inexpensive beginner's musical instrument often used in elementary classrooms to teach children the joys of playing and creating music.

Library

The library is often the nerve center of the school. It is the one room in the school, other than the school cafeteria, where you will find a wide array of topics, students of all ages, and the resources to support any child, any topic, and any project assigned throughout the school. In order to effectively utilize the wide array of resources in the school library, your child will learn several basic research and library skills.

Get your child her very own library card. If you didn't already know, the local library has a wealth of resources available to your child. Not only can you check out books, but also, most libraries have movies, CDs, and books on tape for your use. See if your library hosts a children's Book of the Month Club, a reading group, or any other special productions. Inspire your child to make the most of your library.

Third-grade children are introduced to the anatomy of a book. They learn that there are several parts to a book, including the contents page, title page, and glossary. Children also learn about the way books are arranged and classified in the library, including an introduction to the Dewey decimal system and the encouraged familiarity with the card catalog. Your third grader's budding research skills will be shored by his newly learned ability to use the thesaurus, encyclopedias, atlases, and other research tools. A checklist of skills your third grader may learn this year could include:

➤ Select books from library that match both skill level and interests
➤ Check books out independently and return them in a timely manner
➤ Learn to access online services on computer
➤ Explore Dewey decimal system
➤ Card catalogue utilized independently
➤ Introduced to various research resources

Art

Chances are that your refrigerator is covered with works of art created by your mini-Michelangelo. Art class ranks among the favorites for many elementary students. Unaware of methods and styles being taught to them, they revel in using paints, clay, and paste to create their own masterpieces. The odors of the tempera paints and clay combined with the exclamations of appreciation of a classmate's work are common in school art rooms across the country. In areas where resources allow, children are often able to visit art museums and galleries on short field trips to gain appreciation and knowledge. In schools where cross-curriculum learning is encouraged, children also learn about the historical significance of art. During this year, your third grader may learn to:

➤ Recognize various color schemes as monochromatic and use them in compositions
➤ Understand that changes in light affect the mood of a painting
➤ Use tempera paint in a planned perceived manner, experimenting with various ways to use a paint brush
➤ Understand that details, patterns, and textures may add visual interest to art

➤ Learn imaginative shape and textures in a ceramic artwork
➤ Recognize and use shapes to create pattern and texture
➤ Review how to mix light and dark colors and add values to lights and darks to a painting
➤ Study famous artists

Physical Education

To some children gym class is an added recess tossed into the schedule a couple of days a week, but what they do not realize is that this added thirty to forty minutes of organized play twice each week all has a purpose. Your child is learning, practicing, and refining both fine and large motor skills. He is also gaining an appreciation and knowledge that will encourage him to lead a healthy lifestyle. Other skills taught and encouraged in third-grade physical education class teach children the rewards of following rules, teamwork, and good sportsmanship. All of these are essential for your child's social development, which we discuss in depth in Chapter 4. Some of the games and activities played in third-grade physical education classes are geared to help your child:

➤ Refine running and dodging skills
➤ Refine throwing, catching, punting, dribbling, kicking, and other ball skills
➤ Move rhythmically as individual, or group in action games and activities
➤ Continue developing skills in the Presidential Physical Fitness program
➤ Expand confidence in playing of basic games of football, basketball, soccer
➤ Develop enjoyment for recreational activities such as hoops, ropes, and action games
➤ Demonstrate increased level of performance in stunts, alone and with others
➤ Maintain level of cardiovascular workout during aerobic exercises

The Presidential Physical Fitness program was created to encourage healthy lifestyles, exercise, and achievement in children. For over thirty years children nationwide have been participating in the program. The Presidential Fitness program includes the following activities:

➤ Sit-ups
➤ Pull-ups or push-ups
➤ Sit and reach or trunk flexion
➤ Shuttle run
➤ Mile run

Boys Qualifying Standards are:

AGE	PULL-UPS	SHUTTLE RUN	SIT-UPS	MILE RUN	SIT AND REACH
8	5	11.1 seconds	40	8:48 minutes	31
9	5	10.9 seconds	41	8:31 minutes	31

Girls Qualifying Standards are:

AGE	PULL-UPS	SHUTTLE RUN	SIT-UPS	MILE RUN	SIT AND REACH
8	2	11.8 seconds	38	10:02 minutes	33
9	2	11.1 seconds	39	9:30 minutes	33

Computer

Computer lab classes are also becoming commonplace in elementary schools. Do not be surprised to find your third grader learning basic keyboarding skills along with playing educational games at school.

While in the computer lab, the third grader may work with Macintosh computers or with PCs (commonly known as IBM clones). Fortunately, schools have also become the beneficiaries of rapid advances in technology. While not all schools have the funding to support computer labs, companies often donate outdated, but still functioning computers to school systems. Children may not have the opportunity to work on the latest technology, but it is crucial that they are exposed to computers. Your child should learn how to properly turn on and turn off a computer, how to manipulate a mouse, and how to open and close a program.

Your third grader will also learn about how computers and information technology shape the world around us. Students learn how to create simple graphics, perform word processing skills, and research. Your third grader will learn about features and tools, such as spell check, found within commonly used software to simplify tasks. This familiarity with computers sets the stage for more productivity–based computer use as the child progresses through the higher grades.

While a portion of class time will be spent actually at the keyboard, your third grader will spend some time learning terminology and the basic components of a computer. By the end of the year your third grader should know:

> Basic computer terms such as: mouse, hard drive, monitor, hardware, software, icon, e-mail, etc.
> Basic computer use skills, such as opening a file, saving a file, or creating a new file
> How to use word processing programs such as MS Word or WordPerfect
> How to use software tools, such as spell check, to check for accuracy of work
> How to use graphics and clip art
> Appropriate care and handling procedures for computers, peripherals, and components

Many parents become intimidated by a their child's ability to easily pick up computer skills. If you are unfamiliar with using computers, you will find that your third grader's proficiency and eagerness to "show" what they have learned in school makes him the perfect teacher at home.

STANDARDIZED TESTING

JUST mention standardized testing to a group of parents, and you will receive a myriad of responses. Some will respond like one parent in my community,

"I feel there should be a gentler way to monitor the success of our schools and the progress of our children." Others will accept them as a necessary tool to gauge the effectiveness of our school systems, and there will be others who are vehemently against such mass testing.

One tool that schools use to learn about students is the standardized test. Understanding the role of testing will help you to enable your child to succeed in school and to develop a better relationship between your family and your child's school.

In a brochure written by Carolyn B. Bagin and Lawrence M. Rudner entitled *What Should Parents Know About Standardized Testing in Schools?* many questions are answered, tips offered, and suggestions made. Much of the information offered below is from their brochure.

WHAT ARE STANDARDIZED TESTS?

USUALLY created by commercial test publishers, standardized tests are designed to give a common measure of students' performance. These tests, regardless of where and when they are given, contain the same questions, to be completed in the same amount of time, and are scored in the same way. They give educators a common yardstick or "standard" of measure. Educators use these standardized tests to tell how well school programs are succeeding or to give themselves a picture of the skills and abilities of today's students.

WHY DO SCHOOLS USE STANDARDIZED TESTS?

STANDARDIZED tests can help teachers and administrators make decisions regarding the instructional program. They help schools measure how students in a given class, school, or school system perform in relation to other students who take the same test. Using the results from these tests, teachers and administrators can evaluate the school system, a school program, or a particular student.

HOW DO SCHOOLS USE STANDARDIZED TESTS?

DIFFERENT types of standardized tests have different purposes. Standardized *achievement* tests measure how much students have already learned about a school subject. The results from these tests can help teachers develop programs that suit students' achievement levels in each subject area, such as reading, math, language skills, spelling, or science.

Standardized *aptitude* tests measure students' abilities to learn in school—how well they are likely to do in future school work. Instead of measuring knowledge of subjects taught in school, these tests measure a broad range of abilities or skills that are considered important to success in school. They can measure verbal ability, mechanical ability, creativity, clerical ability, or abstract reasoning. The results from aptitude tests help teachers to plan instruction that is appropriate for the students' levels. Educators most commonly use achievement and aptitude tests to:

➤ Evaluate school programs
➤ Report on students' progress
➤ Diagnose students' strengths and weaknesses
➤ Select students for special programs
➤ Place students in special groups
➤ Certify student achievement (for example, award high school diplomas or promote students from grade to grade)

CAN STANDARDIZED TESTS ALONE DETERMINE MY CHILD'S PLACEMENT IN THE CLASSROOM?

THE answer is no. Paper-and-pencil tests give teachers only part of the picture of your child's strengths and weaknesses. Teachers combine the results of many methods to gain insights into the skills, abilities, and knowledge of your child. These methods include:

➤ Observing students in the classroom
➤ Evaluating their day-to-day class work

➤ Grading their homework assignments
➤ Meeting with their parents
➤ Keeping close track of how students change or grow throughout the year

Standardized tests have limitations. These tests are not perfect measures of what individual students can or cannot do, or of everything students learn. Also, your child's scores on a particular test may vary from day to day, depending on whether your child guesses, receives clear directions, follows the directions carefully, takes the test seriously, and is comfortable in taking the test.

HOW CAN I HELP MY CHILD DO WELL ON TESTS?

HERE are a few suggestions for parents who want to help their children do well on tests.

First and most important, talk to your child's teacher often to monitor your child's progress and find out what activities you can do at home to help your child. Then:

➤ Make sure your child does his or her homework.
➤ Make sure your child is well rested and eats a well-rounded diet.
➤ Have a variety of books and magazines at home to encourage your child's curiosity.
➤ Don't be overly anxious about test scores, but encourage your child to take tests seriously.
➤ Don't judge your child on the basis of a simple test score.

WHAT SHOULD I ASK MY CHILD'S TEACHER?

BEFORE the test . . .

➤ Which tests will be administered during the school year and for what purposes?
➤ Will I be notified about the results?

➤ How will the teacher or the school use the results of the test?
➤ What other means of evaluation will the teacher or the school use to measure your child's performance?
➤ Should your child practice taking tests?

After the test . . .

➤ How do students in your child's school compare with students in other school systems in your state and across the country?
➤ What do the test results mean about your child's skills and abilities?
➤ Are the test results consistent with your child's performance in the classroom?
➤ Are any changes anticipated in your child's educational program?
➤ What can you do at home to help your child strengthen particular skills?

STATES THAT REQUIRE STANDARDIZED TESTING IN THIRD GRADE INCLUDE:

Alabama	Mississippi
Arkansas	Missouri
California	North Carolina
Colorado	Nevada
Delaware	New Hampshire
Florida	New Mexico
Georgia	Oklahoma
Hawaii	Oregon
Illinois	Rhode Island
Indiana	South Carolina
Iowa	Tennessee
Louisiana	Texas
Maryland	Virginia
Massachusetts	Washington, DC
Minnesota	West Viginia

SOME OF THE TESTS GIVEN TO THIRD GRADERS

The Benchmark Exams are given to test the reading, writing, and math skills.

The Colorado Student Assessment Program (CSAP) tests only reading skills.

The Delaware Student Testing Program (DSTP) tests reading, writing, and math skills.

The Florida Comprehensive Assessment Test (FCAT) tests third graders' reading and math skills.

The Illinois Standards Achievement Test (ISAT) assesses reading, writing, and math skills.

The Iowa Test of Basic Skills (ITBS) is offered in a variety of states to evaluate reading, writing, and math skills.

The Iowa Tests of Educational Development (ITED) are given in various states to assess reading, writing, math, social studies, and science knowledge.

The Maryland School Performance Assessment Program (MSPAP) tests students in the subjects of reading, writing, and math.

The Massachusetts Comprehensive Assessment System tests reading skills only.

The Minnesota Comprehensive Assessment (MCAP) tests reading and math.

The Missouri Assessment Program (MAP) tests third graders' writing and science skills.

The New Hampshire Educational Improvement and Assessment (NHEIA) offers reading and math tests to third graders.

The New Mexico Achievement Assessment is given to third graders to test reading, writing, and math skills.

The North Carolina Testing Program tests reading and math.

The Oregon Statewide Assessment tests reading, writing, and math skills.

The Palmetto Achievement Challenge Test (PACT) is given to South Carolina third graders to test their reading, writing, and math skills.

The Stanford Achievement Test (SAT) is not to be confused with the college entrance exam. This tests students' skills in reading, writing, mathematics, and spelling.

The Terra Nova test assesses reading, writing, math, social studies, and science.

The Texas Assessment of Academic Skills (TAAS) tests reading and math.

CLOSING NOTES ON CURRICULUM

As you see, the third grader has a lot of learning to do this year. A majority of the time the third-grade student will be concentrating on Reading and Language Arts skills geared toward helping him understand and communicate more clearly. Across the entire curriculum reading and the understanding of what has been read are key to your child's educational success. This will be the last year in your child's schooling where reading is emphasized to such a high degree, so take advantage of all the tools and resources, and the teacher's willingness to help your child succeed.

The curriculum samples provided are similar to those used across the United States. Your child's third-grade curriculum will probably not contain all of the skills and goals outlined here. Most likely, your child's curriculum will contain a few of the major skills mentioned as well as some skills not mentioned. To be best prepared for third grade, contact your local school, or log on to your school's website to research your individual school's curriculum.

Your child will have his own set of unique talents and skills. It is important that, although a curriculum is based on the average student, you recognize your child's strengths and weaknesses within your school's curriculum to ensure his educational success. You can also learn more about how to supplement your child's learning by turning the pages and reading Chapter 3.

3

How to Supplement What Your Child Is Learning

YOUR involvement in your child's education is one of the most precious gifts you can give to him. He will learn from you, follow your example, and emulate your attitude. You will be setting the stage for his success. The teachers in your child's school spend their days teaching approximately twenty children per classroom the subjects set forth in the school's curriculum. When your third grader gets home to you, it is time to let him shine. With your one-on-one attention, he will be able to further enjoy his favorite subjects, get the help with the subjects he is struggling with, and know that you are a willing partner in his education.

Your involvement also allows your child to feel comfortable discussing the day's events and lessons with you. Show interest in what your child is doing at school. If you do not show interest, she may soon quit wanting to share. It is imperative for your child's growth that those lines of communication remain open. This communication also affords you the opportunity to hear the unspoken. If your third grader never mentions what is going on in math class, you may want to broach the subject yourself. Her omission of math class in discussion may mean that she is disinterested, bored, or having difficulty.

Sometimes we parents feel so intimidated by the new methods of teaching and learning that we may shy away from helping our children with their schoolwork. Remember that you do not have to be an expert in any given subject to help your child study or become more interested. There are bound to be some topics covered in your child's education that you are unfamiliar with. Push up your sleeves, wipe your brow, and get ready to learn. It looks as though there is an opportunity for you to learn something new as well. Your child will revel in the opportunity to "teach" you something. He will be anxious to research a topic so that the two of you learn together. It is important that you understand that you are not expected to have the IQ of Einstein, just the energy and the interest to be a good role model, involved parent, and willing listener. If you possess those qualities, you are well prepared to provide your child with a healthy learning environment.

Because raising successful children requires parents to support one another, I asked many parents for some fun tips that they use to supplement their child's learning. Below you will find a list of some of the activities and tips they offered that could help you foster your child's interest in learning. Not only are activities like these important for your child's academic success, but also they offer the opportunity for communication that is not possible during the normal chaos of the day.

READING/LANGUAGE ARTS

AS we have learned in the previous chapter, Reading and Language Arts dominate the third grader's schedule. Your third grader's best chance of success comes with your support of his reading activities.

Be sure to take time to read aloud to your third grader. Although he is getting older, bigger, more independent, and less cuddlesome, he still enjoys spending time sitting with you reading chapter books. Perhaps you could read a portion of the book to him one night, and he could read a portion of the book to you the next evening.

"I have a nine-year-old who . . . loves to read. And she also loves to be read to—and I'm just discovering this. I thought she had "outgrown" this because she knows how to read, but I was wrong. We have been making a move this summer and found some of her old favorites— *Ramona, Charlotte's Web, Pippi Longstocking, Stuart Little,* etc."

—A TEACHER AND PARENT OF A THIRD GRADER FROM ILLINOIS

➤ Read aloud to your child: books, newspaper and magazine articles, the back of the cereal box, labels on cans, or directions.
➤ Read poems aloud together to learn about rhythm and repeated sounds in language.
➤ Establish a reading time, even if it's only 10 minutes each day. Make sure there is a good reading light in your child's room and stock her bookshelves with books and magazines that are easy to both read and reach.
➤ Listen to your child read homework or favorite stories to you every day.
➤ Go to the library together and check out books. Be sure to ask the librarian for good books or to help you find what you need.
➤ Have books, magazines, and papers around the house and let your child see that you like to read, too.
➤ Encourage older children to read to younger children.
➤ Help experienced readers talk and write about what they read.

Encourage activities that require reading. Cooking (reading a recipe), constructing a kite (reading directions), or identifying a bird's nest or a shell at the beach (reading a reference book) are some examples.

Activities

Reading Signs
While on a car trip, take turns reading billboards. If your trip includes a familiar route, make a list of words that you know are on the route. Encourage your child to play this game of word "hide and seek."

And That's the End of the Story . . .

Improve listening skills and imagination. Read a story aloud to your child and stop before the end. Ask the child, "What do you think is going to happen next?" Then finish the story and discuss the ending with the child. Did it turn out the way you thought?

Journal Writing

Encourage journal writing at home as well as at school. Provide your third grader with a notebook, pencils, and quiet place where he can keep his thoughts. Be a good role model; start a journal yourself. Document your third grader's growth. Both journals will become treasured keepsakes for years to come.

Reading and Writing

1. Reading and writing go hand in hand. Have your child read school assignments aloud.
2. Explain that when you read, you should listen to how the writing sounds by asking yourself

   - Does the writing sound like the way people talk?
   - Is it smooth or choppy?
   - Are there any words or ideas missing?
   - How could the writing be made more interesting? By adding descriptions, using examples, going into more detail with explanations?

3. Encourage your child to read with expression, emphasizing the words in the sentences that are most important to your child.
4. Encourage others who might be listening to ask questions about the writing.

Learn about Folk Tales

Retell tales through dramatic play. Find out more about your family's own background. Here's all you need:

➤ A folktale book, such as *Anansi the Spider*, an African folk tale about a spider who has six sons. Anansi goes on a journey and subsequently finds himself in trouble. His sons each help him, but when it comes to the reward, a beautiful globe of light, he can't decide to which son it should go. Instead, Anansi puts the globe of light in to the sky (the moon), for all to enjoy.

Directions:

➤ Read the book, in this case *Anansi the Spider*. Anansi is a legendary spider. He is the keeper of all of the folk tales in a certain African culture. How did he get this job? What can you learn from this story?
➤ Act out the story of Anansi. Practice your performance.
➤ Explain that in Africa, this is how some cultures pass on stories: they perform it for young children.
➤ Find other folk tales from your culture. Have a librarian help you. Act it out for family and friends at Thanksgiving.

Junk Mail Turned Fun Mail

Instead of tossing that junk mail, use it as a learning tool. Have your child go through it to find letters, sight words, spelling words, and reading words.

MATH

Suddenly the world of numbers has opened up for your third grader. He now realizes that he can manipulate numbers; make them work for him. Building a good mathematical foundation starts now. You will want to make math as fun as possible so that your third grader will grow to become an adult who is very comfortable and successful with math.

General Tips

➤ Show your children that you like numbers. Play number games and think of math problems as puzzles to be solved.
➤ From the time your child is very young, count everything. When you empty a grocery bag, count the number of apples. Count the number of stairs to your home.
➤ Put things into groups. When you do laundry, separate items of clothing: all the socks in one pile, shirts in another, and pants in another. Divide the socks by color and count the number of each.

Draw pictures and graphs of clothes in the laundry: 4 red socks, 10 blue socks, 12 white socks.

➤ Tell your children that anyone can learn math. Point out numbers in your child's life: in terms of weight, measurements involving cooking, temperature, and time.

➤ Help your children do math in their heads with lots of small numbers. Ask questions: "If I have 4 cups and I need 7, how many more do I need?" or "If I need 12 drinks for the class, how many packages of 3 drinks will I need?"

Activities

Board Games

Have you ever played Yahtzee® with your children? This is a fun and effective way to teach children their early multiplication facts. Did you know that the game of Yahtzee only costs approximately five dollars at most discount department stores? What a fun, inexpensive way to memorize your multiplication tables.

Your third grader will also be spending time learning how mathematics affects his real life situations. One of the units covered in math this year will address money, how to recognize and count the various denominations. Playing board games with your third grader, such as Payday, Monopoly Jr., Life, and other money–based games allows your third grader to pretend he is the "banker" in charge of doling out money. He will also learn to pay the bank "rent" for his properties and other life expenses.

Food Fun

When preparing a snack or meal, cut foods, such as a slice of bread, an apple or orange, into equal parts and talk about fractions with your child. If you have an 8–slice pizza, and there are four people in your family, how many slices of pizza are there for each person in your family?

Number Navigator

The drives to Grandpa's house, or to the "not-so-local" shopping mall were enhanced when we played "airplane." I was the pilot, following the instructions from my navigator. We would pretend that we were talking into headsets, and used the "roger, over and out" to simulate that our vehicle was really an airplane. This taught geography, cartography, and memory skills. As my oldest got better at this game, we added gas mileage and time to the mixture. For instance, "Ross, we are traveling 50 miles per hour and have 25 miles to travel until we get to Grandpa's. How long until we get there." You would be amazed at how quickly children learn the time/speed relationships. They do not even realize they are learning because it is all under the guise of a game.

Money Match—A Game

1. The object of the game is to be the first player to earn a set amount (for example, 20 or 50 cents).
2. Each player rolls the dice and gets the amount of pennies that the number on the dice shows.
3. As each player gets 5 pennies, a nickel replaces the pennies, and a dime replaces 10 pennies or 2 nickels.
4. The first player to reach the set amount wins.

Critter Counting

Buy a white dry-erase board—and many, many markers. Place the board on the floor or table and have the children gather around it. Do math problems using critters as the subject. Ask your child to draw a cat with a litter of kittens. When the child has drawn the animals, you can pretend to come and "buy" (erase) some of the kittens. If the kittens were 7 dollars each, how much did I owe her? How much could she expect to get from those left? You can pretend to buy supplies, such as food (cereal is a great fill-in) for the kittens. This game appeals to visual, tactile, and kinesthetic learners.

Origami

Fractions can be an art form. Go to your local craft store and pick up an origami kit. Without cutting, gluing, or decorating, your child will create forms and animals by folding. Your child will learn to fold the paper into halves, quarters, and sixteenths to create anything from a frog to a swan.

Test Preparedness

If your third grader is having difficulty with math facts, such as multiplication tables, create your own "pretests" at home. Follow a format similar to the test that your child's teacher uses. This will be a great drill for those cumbersome multiplication tables, and will calm some of those "test nerves."

Pop!

A favorite game around my house is "Pop!" We choose a number; lets say three (3). We then take turns counting. Any number with the number three as one of the digits, or is divisible by the number three is represented by "Pop!" For example:

> Player 1: "one"
> Player 2: "two"
> Player 3: "Pop!"—This number (3) would be both divisible by three, and have the number three as a digit
> Player 4: "four"
> Player 1: "five"
> Player 2: "Pop!"—This number (6) is divisible by three
> Player 3: "seven"
> Player 4: "eight"

This game usually provides us with a lot of laughs and is easily played in the car while zipping to and from the little league field.

"My nine-year-old son loves to cook and bake, so . . . to make the recipe a little more difficult we don't just take the recipe from the card. We make 1 1/2 times the recipe! That takes some math to figure out how much of each ingredient is needed. When we go shopping, we figure

the tax on any item that he purchases BEFORE checking out. It's a great game to see if we are correct with our math."

—A MOM FROM WASHINGTON

SOCIAL STUDIES

MUCH of your third grader's social studies will focus on government and American history. Encouraging and supporting our third graders in social studies can be fun. Many events in history can be told to your child as a mystery suspense story. If you get into character, it can be even more fun.

Some General Tips

➤ Share family history with your children. Share your memories, and help your relatives and friends share family stories, too. Encourage your children to tell their own stories.

➤ Read historically based stories to your child. Was the story accurate? Was it fact or fiction?

➤ Watch television programs about topics related to the past with your children. Get library books on the same topics. Do the books and television programs agree?

➤ When you celebrate holidays explain to your child what is being celebrated and why. Help your child find stories or speeches about these holidays at the library or in a newspaper or magazine.

➤ Visit a local battlefield, historical home, or other significant landmark with your child.

➤ Get to know the history of the town or city where you live. Your newspaper may list parades, museum and art exhibits, children's theater, music events, history talks and walks under "things to do." Choose some of these activities to do with your children.

➤ Attend festivals and fairs sponsored by a variety of ethnic, cultural, and community organizations.

➤ Make globes, maps, and encyclopedias available, and use every opportunity to refer to them. A reference to China in a child's favorite story, or the red, white, and green stripes on a box of spaghetti can be opportunities to learn more about the world.

Activities

Where Am I?

Find a map of your community. First find the approximate location of your house, then your street, and then find some familiar landmarks, such as the firehouse, grocery store, or school.

GREAT IDEA!

I Wish . . .

Make a wish list of places your child would like to visit. Look them up on a map or globe. Take the time to learn about the history, the food, or the tourist sites of that place. If your child wishes to travel to a foreign country, discuss the ways in which to get there. Could you drive to Japan? How did people get from Europe to the United States before there were airplanes? Ask other relevant questions about what she thinks life is like in that country. Or what language she thinks the people there speak. Your child will begin to think about the world beyond her neighborhood.

Mealtime Learning

Prepare an ethnic dish with your third grader. This can be as simple as an Asian stir fry or a Mexican fiesta. While preparing and enjoying the meal, discuss the culture of the country and background of the dish. If the dish has particular historical significance (such as Thanksgiving Day turkey), be sure to include that in the discussion.

Crossing the Line

While on a car trip and crossing state lines, name the state capital and other pertinent information about that state. These facts could include state flower, important cities, landmarks, and historical events. You can play a variation of this game by scouting for out-of-state license plates.

SCIENCE

FORTUNATELY science fills the world around us. With the correct guidance, most third graders enjoy learning about science as it pertains to their world. Engage your child; get him involved.

General Tips

➤ Ask your children questions: How do you think the clock works? Why does a bird make a nest and what is the nest made of? How does the sun help us every day?

➤ Have children look at what's happening around them and have them write down what they see.

➤ Have your children make predictions about the weather or how fast a plant will grow or how high a piece of paper will fly with the wind. Have your children then test to see if their hunches are correct.

➤ Remind your child that it may take many tries before you get an answer. Keep trying.

➤ Have your children start collections of shells, rocks, or bugs, so that they can see similarities and patterns.

➤ Have your child look at how things are different. He or she can look around the neighborhood to see the different animals and plants that live and grow there.

➤ Help your child look at what causes things to change. What happens when a plant doesn't have water or sunlight?

Activities

Scavenger Hunt
See if you can find . . .

➤ A simple machine
➤ A footprint made by an animal
➤ Something changed by the sun

➤ Something changed by the rain

➤ An animal that would fit inside a coffee cup

➤ One of thc bodies of the Solar System

➤ Something that does not smell nice

➤ An example of pollution

➤ An insect

Build a Weather Center

Pick up a rain gauge and thermometer at a local hardware store. Create a simple chart where your third grader can chart the temperature, precipitation, and other weather facts (such as how sunny or windy it is). Watch the local weather forecast with him to help verify his weather facts. Discuss the meteorologist's weather map, and then try your hands at forecasting the next day's weather. Also, after you have charted the weather for a few weeks, discuss trends, and your accuracy at forecasting.

Make Your Own Satellite

You will need some everyday recyclable items such as tin foil, Styrofoam cups or bowls, plastic bottles, plastic containers, milk cartons, and empty paper towel rolls, as well as any other items you can scavenge. You will also need tools such as scissors, tape, glue, markers, etc. Using these items, let your third grader's imagination go wild! You may be nurturing a future aerospace engineer.

Grow Vegetables and Herbs in Your Home—All Year Round

Here's all you need:

➤ vegetable and herb seeds or seedlings, such as parsley, chives, garlic, scallions, basil, oregano, patio tomatoes, cabbage, lettuce, carrots, or radishes

➤ potting soil mixture

➤ cut down milk cartons, jars, lids, food packaging, egg shells in three-quarter pieces or larger

Directions:

- ➤ Avocados: Remove the pit. Insert toothpicks to secure the pit so that it is half-emerged, in a glass of water. When roots sprout, plant in soil.
- ➤ Lemon, orange, lime seeds: Place four or five seeds in a container. Cover with a layer of soil. Place containers under a large jar until you see sprouts. Remove jar. Place in sunny window.
- ➤ Sweet potatoes: Place in a carton. Keep potato half-covered with water
- ➤ Carrots: Cut the green top. Place in a jar lid filled with water. Watch the greens grow!
- ➤ Grass or bird seeds: Place on a wet sponge in a dish. Keep sponge moist. Seeds will sprout!
- ➤ Cress: Grow sprouts in an eggshell. Green sprouts will look like hair coming out. Draw a face and body.
- ➤ Talk about farming and how important it was to the early settlers.
- ➤ Discuss where food from the grocery store is grown today.
- ➤ Reflect on how lucky we are to have so much food available.

Recycle!

Take your child with you on your weekly trip to the recycling center. Learn where the objects you sorted are taken and what new products are made from them.

CURSIVE WRITING

YOUR child will learn the basics of cursive writing in class through exercises and practice. If you notice that your child is having difficulty with the slanting, looping cursive letters, you may want to reinforce what he has learned at school with practice sessions at home. Have some lined paper handy—you can find handwriting paper at most discount stores. You will also want to keep an ample supply of sharpened pencils. By this time your third grader is probably used to standard #2 pencils. To encourage good handwriting:

Letters in the Sand

Have your child practice difficult letters by tracing her index finger over sandpaper letters, or by writing the forms in the air, on a table-top, or in the sandbox. Encourage large hand movements at first, gradually moving toward fine motor movements as she improves.

➤ Avoid comparing your child's handwriting with siblings, or friends. Criticism can dampen your child's desire to want to improve.
➤ Let your third grader "write" letters with his finger on your back. Try to guess what letter he is writing.
➤ When your third grader is doing homework, encourage him to take his time to write neatly.

FOREIGN LANGUAGE

NOT all schools offer foreign language in third grade. If your school does, you should feel very lucky. Knowing a foreign language is becoming more and more important as many cultures are defined not by the boundaries of their lands, but by their heritage. Although you may feel very intimidated with the idea of helping your third grader with a foreign language, remember that you are not expected to know about everything, you are only expected to be supportive. Many of the words that your child will be learning in his foreign language class have everyday usage. Allow your child to count oranges in his newly learned language. Let him practice his pronunciation by teaching you how to count. Go to the library and check out books or language tapes so that you can become more familiar with the foreign language.

Bilingual Books

Find a copy of the classic, *Goodnight Moon*. Because this is an easy reader that your child is likely to know by heart, it is a perfect way to introduce books in other languages. Find the same book in Spanish translation (available at Amazon.com) and have your child read it. Your child will be able to pick up on the meanings of the words in Spanish because he will already know what they are in English. This is a great way to get your child interested in foreign languages.

MUSIC

CHANCES are that your third grader loves to sing and dance. His casual love of music is endearing as he belts out the latest song from the radio. He will sing songs learned at school, songs heard around the house, and commercial jingles.

General Tips

Some ways to encourage your musical eight-year-old are:

➤ Provide your child with a wide array of music at home. Listen to all types of music—popular, classical, jazz, country, folk, and opera.
➤ Take your third grader to live musical performances. This could include choral concerts, religious events, or live performances.
➤ Converse in song. Hold a conversation with your third grader by singing to him; encourage him to respond in song as well.
➤ Make up silly lyrics to familiar tunes.
➤ If possible, encourage instrumental lessons, such as piano.
➤ Play clapping, dancing, and drumming games.
➤ Enroll your third grader in dance lessons.
➤ For a fun weekend, rent a musical, such as *The Sound of Music* or *Annie*.

Disc Jockey

Along with your child, sort your CD collection by musical type, or performer. Discuss the musician and the music with her while you sort. As a reward, allow her to choose CDs along the way to listen to, allowing her to associate the musical type with the artist.

LIBRARY

Activities

WHILE your third grader will look forward to weekly trips to the school library, he will look forward to visiting the library with you as well. Take your third grader to the local library, get him his own card, and share your local public library. While at the library, you may want to sign him up for some of the reading programs offered by the library. Many times public libraries schedule Saturday morning reading sessions, or summer events for their young readers.

General Tips

- ➤ Include children in trips to the library, and go often.
- ➤ As soon as you can, help your child get a library card.
- ➤ Borrow recordings of children's stories and songs, cassette tapes, compact discs, videotapes, even puppets, and educational toys.
- ➤ Find out if your library has computers and how your children can use them to learn or upgrade skills.
- ➤ Encourage your children to use the library to find information for their homework.
- ➤ Encourage your children to ask for help from you and the librarian in finding books and materials.
- ➤ Work with the librarian to teach older children how to find things in the library on their own.
- ➤ Teach your children how to take care of themselves in public places, especially if they use the library alone. Stress common sense guidelines for behavior in the library.

Play Librarian

Many children have a collection of books in their room. Have your child sort and organize her books, pretending she is the librarian. Have her make "library cards" and keep track of books she lends out to her brothers, sisters, and friends. She will also learn to care for her books and to keep them where she can find them.

GREAT IDEA!

ART

MOST of us have been encouraging our child's inner artist since she was old enough to hold onto a crayon. Now she may have an art kit, easel, and markers at her disposal, along with a kit of watercolors. Be sure to keep an appropriate amount of art supplies on hand. Some children may require paints and chalks as well as crayons and markers.

General Tips

➤ Let your child express himself. A picture doesn't have to look like something you can recognize.
➤ Have your child talk about the picture to describe what it is supposed to be. This helps develop language skills.
➤ Encourage your child to make patterns of repeated colors and shapes. This helps develop an understanding of math.
➤ Have your child practice different techniques: create with soft lines, create with blocks of color, create using different media.
➤ Have your child make connections between artwork and other subjects. Look at, and talk about book illustrations when you are reading together.
➤ Check art books out of the library and look at famous paintings. Talk about what is in the picture and how the artist painted it (did he use thick paint with bold strokes or did she use light colors with dots of paint?).
➤ Display your child's art in your home and office.

Activities

Life-Sized Creation

1. Stretch out a large sheet of paper. If you do not have a large roll of paper, you could ask your local butcher for a piece of butcher paper, or visit your local art supply store.
2. Trace around your third grader's body.
3. Give him crayons, markers, and colored pencils and other art supplies to fill in the details, such as clothes, eyes, nose, mouth, etc.

Sidewalk Chalk Fun

Supplies necessary: Sidewalk chalk, and a large plot of sidewalk or driveway.

Let your third grader's mind wander in the sidewalk chalk. Encourage play learning, for instance. He could draw a small town on which to drive his miniature cars and trucks.

Art from Stuff

1. Go on a treasure hunt outside to find things that could be used in a collage; a picture where shapes and colors are pasted on a piece of paper or cardboard: sticks and leaves, flowers to be pressed, feathers, berries to be crushed to use as paint, pebbles, shells.
2. Go on a treasure hunt inside to find other things such as scraps of paper, buttons, pieces of cloth, or ribbon.
3. Look for some heavy cardboard or wood to use as a backing.
4. Have your child lay out the materials in a design on the backing. Have your child move things around until the design is what she wants.
5. Using heavy-duty glue, have your child glue the items on the backing.

PHYSICAL EDUCATION

ALTHOUGH all of us know that each child is different, you may notice that your third grader is hitting a growth spurt. Suddenly he is stretching out, becoming a bit gangly and lean. An active third grader is likely to be a happy third grader. All children have different body types and energy levels. Understand that although your child may not be a naturally gifted athlete, he will benefit from physical activity, team sports, and exercise.

There are many ways that you can build upon your child's awareness of physical education, health, safety, and fitness.

General Tips

➤ Get involved in intramural sports programs at your school, YMCA/YWCA, or Community Center.

➤ Swimming lessons are often available at community centers or schools. Do sign your child up for those classes. It is not only a matter of fitness, but of safety as well.

➤ Provide opportunities at home to play and exercise.

➤ Limit TV time to encourage other more physical activities.

➤ Encourage participation in team sports such as Little League baseball and the American Youth Soccer Organization (AYSO).

➤ Encourage your child's interest in individual sports, such as tennis or golf.

➤ Encourage good hygiene habits

➤ Be a good role model. Exercise regularly, take walks, and practice healthy habits.

Invent a Sport

GREAT IDEA!

Use your child's physical strengths to invent a sport at which she can excel. Make up a name for your sport or game and decide on what equipment is needed to play. Is it a team sport, or do you play alone? Be creative, you can also make up silly rules such as, every time you score a goal, you have to yell, "chicken feathers." If your child is not the most athletic, the silliness combined with physical activity will allow her to be comfortable playing her newly invented sport.

COMPUTER

I T has become more and more evident over the past five years that the more familiar our children are with computers, the better. Computers have permeated our libraries, schools, and finally our homes. Having a home computer gives your child the leg up to understanding and using a computer for fun, learning, and productivity tasks. Studies have shown that children with access to computers perform at a higher level than those who don't.

If you do not already own a computer, you may want to consider making this purchase now. When shopping for a computer for your child, you will want to be familiar with these terms: RAM, hard drive, modem, floppy disk drive, CD-ROM.

Unless you will be giving the computer to the family for a special event (such as Christmas or birthday gift), include your children in the purchase process. You would be surprised how much they can tell you about computers.

G R E A T   I D E A !

Computers Are Everywhere

Even if you don't have a computer in your home, show your child how computers are used in the world around them. Show them the cash register at the grocery store, the computers at the bank, and perhaps the computer you use at the office. All of these types of computers help make our daily lives easier and more efficient.

Provide your child with interesting, educational activities to do on the computer. When purchasing computer software, read the box and be sure you are purchasing software for your child's abilities, not for your child's age. Ask other parents and friends for advice. They will know which computer and which software worked for them. Large warehouse–type stores often stock a large variety of educational software at very affordable prices. Check out the Resources section for LearningExpress's recommendations.

If you are unable to purchase a computer for your home, try to schedule some computer time with your child at a local library. You may also want to sign up for a summer computer workshop for yourself, your child, or both of you. Some schools offer summer computer camps, sign up now.

If you have a home computer, and are connected to the Internet, you will want to cover safety rules with your third grader. They need to know that they should:

➤ Never use the Internet without your permission
➤ Never give out personal information such as their name, address, school, phone number, etc.
➤ Never give out your personal information
➤ Never give out passwords
➤ Only go to sites that you have given your stamp of approval
➤ Always ask you for help finding sites for a research project

See the Resources section for a list of safe and informative websites for your third grader.

GENERAL TIPS—ACROSS THE CURRICULUM

THERE ARE many ways to encourage and supplement your child's learning at home. There are some tips and ideas that don't fit into just one subject, but will help your child across the entire curriculum, and throughout life.

Be a good role model. You are your child's first teacher. He will become energized with your willingness to immerse yourself in third-grade science or math. He will bask in your knowledge of social studies. He will enjoy listening to your voice as you read his favorite story to him. From you, he will learn how to make mistakes, and gracefully recover. Remember how important you are to your child. Even when you are not working on schoolwork, you are your child's hero.

Recognize your child's learning personality. All children are different, it is important that you recognize your child's unique learning style and tailor your supplemental learning situations to fit his style. A child who is not a good reader, but loves hands-on learning will learn much more from searching for insects than he will from reading about insects.

Get your child involved. Choose an organization or two to enroll your child in. This could be a church group or perhaps scouting. These organizations often teach children life lessons that supplement some of the topics covered in school. Scouts often learn about science, safety, and hygiene. They also learn about the world around them. This fun, outside-of-school environment allows for your child to succeed without the pressures of the school environment.

Become familiar with your child's textbooks and learning materials. You will be better able to understand your child's learning and his tasks if you are familiar with his learning materials. Take the time to look through his textbooks and notebooks.

Provide educational materials at home. Be sure to include at least one educational gift on birthdays, Christmas, or Hanukkah. Some educational gifts include: books, software, board games, workbooks, or art supplies.

SUMMARY

PROVIDE tools for success. There are certain tools and supplies that your third grader will require in order for him to complete his lessons well. Be sure to have an ample supply of pencils, paper, and crayons at home. You will also want to have a ruler, some glue or paste, and a pair of scissors. Because your child will be carrying a lot of books and papers to and from school, a comfortable backpack or book bag is also necessary.

Be a willing participant in your child's education. There are so many opportunities to teach your child; they pop up everyday without even thinking about them. You do not have to be rich; you do not have to live in a specific town or city. You only have to be willing, a bit creative, and be prepared to transform even the most mundane task or situation into a learning experience. Making learning fun will stimulate your child's imagination and willingness to learn.

Learning is done year-round, all-day, everyday. Learning opportunities present themselves daily. Encourage learning activities, even if it is by way of games or play. Sometimes play learning is the most effective. Eventually your child will begin to recognize these opportunities herself and will present you with the challenges.

4

Your Child's Social Development

YOUR child grows and changes immensely in third grade. You may miss the chubby cheeked little person that you sent off to kindergarten just a few short years ago. He will be replaced by a taller, lankier, and more self-confident young person. You will also notice many differences in your child socially and emotionally. This is the grade of spreading wings. Whereas the five-year-old that you sent to kindergarten might have had a difficult time paying attention to a task or topic for more than a few minutes, your third grader may have the ability to remain focused for more than twenty minutes. Many parents find that third grade is a wonderful year because their child is less needy than in previous years, and thinks and acts more independently. Other parents become frustrated because that same independence is sometimes accompanied by some of the less pleasant residuals of peer pressure. Your child's unique personality is forming, and is more openly exhibited at this age than any previous school year. Understanding the emotional and social makeup of the common third grader allows you to be prepared for some of the issues that may come your way over the next year.

Most third graders are eager to please their parents, teachers, and peers. Although, throughout previous grades, parents and teachers held the top spots on the list of those a child strove to please, this year's list is beginning to shift. The third grader is becoming more aware and more concerned about those in his peer group. It is very important to him to be viewed with approval by his friends and classmates. Your child will struggle to balance his willingness to please adults with his need to impress his peers. He wants to please the adults in his life, but he's equally interested in gaining the respect of his peers, and unfortunately the two do not always go hand in hand. For this reason, the third grader may be very cautious. For example, an unsure third grader will shy away from answering questions in class for two reasons—he does not want to disappoint his teacher with an incorrect answer, and he does not want to be perceived as a "know-it-all" by his peers.

THE INDEPENDENT CHILD

THE third grader will begin to learn about goals, and will strive to meet those goals with the assistance of a teacher or parent. She will occasionally bite off more than she can chew, so to speak. Her self-expectations may be set unreachably high, and this can lead to frustration. The know-it-all attitude that becomes commonplace in third grade will make it hard for your third grader to ask for help. If she is left to struggle with an unrealistic goal, she will become frustrated and unhappy.

In third grade, the rules change. My son has told us that he doesn't want to be treated like a little kid anymore. He also wants his own alarm clock to get him up when school starts back this August. He thinks that he's too big to be awakened by his mom anymore. I wasn't expecting him to feel this way till at least the age of ten. It seems that kids are trying to grow up faster nowadays. I think that my son has had to face things at a younger age than I did.

—A MOM FROM CONNECTICUT

Because of her predisposal to self-criticism and her innate need to display her newfound independence, she will need your assistance in setting realistic goals. Large projects may require your special attention. Teaching her to break a large project into smaller pieces will not only provide her with the basic principles of time management and organization, but also will allow her to succeed at many small goals instead of struggling with a single obstacle.

While helping your child organize her time, and prioritize her tasks, remember that her capabilities have improved drastically this year. Her attention span has greatly improved—she may be able to work independently and remain focused for an extended period of time. Her abilities to explore and research have also improved drastically. She will work at a furious pace, anxious to learn more while completing a project. It is very likely that you will need to step in to slow your third grader down. If you do not, you may find that her work is sloppy. If the task is a written assignment, her penmanship may be barely legible. She will write quickly, without thought for neatness. Her entire mindset will be to get the job done, no matter how careless she is. She will require you to keep her at a realistic pace, and to remind her not to be careless.

Another hallmark of this year is the third grader's sudden feeling of always being right. Suddenly your third grader will have a huge array of opinions, and will feel very sure that each of his opinions is correct. Sometimes he will become very angry or agitated if others do not agree with these thoughts and opinions.

If You Can't Say Something Nice . . . .

Children at this age tend to have very strong opinions. Explain to your child that everything he thinks does not have to come out of his mouth as speech. Encourage him to have opinions that he also keeps to himself. For example, if he has an opinion about a school subject that he likes, encourage him to express himself. However, if he feels the need to comment on how ugly he thinks his sister's shirt is, it might be better left unsaid.

Also, remember to explain that opinions are not fact. People can have different opinions. It does not mean that one is right and the other wrong. Tell him that it's OK for someone else to be right, or to just have a different opinion.

GREAT IDEA!

The newly discovered sense of self and of goals leads to another new concept—responsibility. The third grader is learning to take charge of his own possessions and to be held accountable for his actions. Responsibility is stressed this year in school, when teachers are expecting a child to complete and turn in homework, forms, and assignments by deadlines. Many third graders struggle with being responsible for themselves and their property. They will forget to return assignments, lose forms in the dark vast expanses of their desks, and have the proverbial "dog ate my homework" type of responses. As a parent, be aware of your child's responsibility strengths and weaknesses. Some ways that you can help hone these skills are:

➤ Provide tools, such as assignment books and binders to assist him
➤ Assign chores around the house to teach responsibility and tasking
➤ Be a good role model: be on time for appointments, always have forms completed
➤ Ask your child each evening if he has materials to return to school

THE EMOTIONAL ROLLER COASTER

THIRD grade is hard work, especially given the emotional growth your child is experiencing. Endearing smiles, silly antics, and serious brooding mark this year's child. You may be kept off-balance wondering which one of your child's personalities will come home from school each day.

Tears are common during this year, so are smiles; big smiles with missing front teeth. These are the smiles of which your favorite snapshots are made. Most of the time your third grader will be quite pleasant, laughing, playing, and conversing. A newly found interest in humor and jokes often rears itself this year. You may find yourself exhausted by the plethora of jokes your budding comedian feels compelled to try out on you.

Your third grader may be become a puddle of tears for no apparent reason. Sometimes you may become frustrated, wondering why the tears flow so easily from your otherwise happy child. She may emotionally breakdown at the drop of a hat, at the most inopportune times. Although you may find your cheeks reddening, and your temperature soaring as your third grader melts down in the middle of a crowd, remember that we have all worn those shoes.

Although your first reaction may be to wonder why your child is acting more like a five-year-old than an eight- or nine-year-old, it is important that you handle the situation with understanding, caring, and an even temper. During the meltdown, try not to focus on those around you witnessing your uncomfortable situation. Focus instead on your third grader, and what circumstances could have triggered the meltdown. Consider the events of the day. Is your child overtired? Is she struggling with a new task at home or at school? Perhaps her meltdown was triggered by something as simple as being a hungry. Evaluate the situation while allowing your third grader to escape with her self-esteem intact.

SELF-ESTEEM

AH, there is that phrase! I am sure you were wondering how far you would make it through this book before we would talk about self-esteem. Unfortunately, we are all so familiar with the term self-esteem that it sometimes loses its sense of importance. The truth of the matter is that nurturing a child's self-esteem now will only pay off a hundred fold in the future.

Self-esteem has been studied for over a hundred years. Experts are not sure exactly when in the development process that self-esteem begins to become important, but almost all experts, parents, and teachers agree that good self-esteem is key to raising successful, happy children.

What Is Self-Esteem?

Self-esteem can be defined as the feelings one has about themselves. Those feelings, good or bad, have a deep effect on how a person carries him- or herself, how they see themselves, and the level of effort they are willing to put into their own success.

A person who is constantly degrading him- or herself, finding fault with their work, or is overly skeptical of themselves is said to have low self-esteem. Generally they don't feel good about themselves, and therefore they have a difficult time feeling good about the world around them. Children with low self-esteem tend to feel as though they are unimportant to the adults in their lives.

They often feel as though those same adults would be happier without them around. This leads to the child feeling insecure, unsafe, and often unloved. Low self-esteem also can contribute to low test scores, low energy level, and poor behavior.

On the other hand, a person who sets realistic goals for him- or herself, feels comfortable about their accomplishments, and is happy with their situation in life is said to have good self-esteem. The person with good, or high self-esteem finds happiness in the world around them. Children with good self-esteem feel very important to the adults around them. They feel safe and secure. The child believes that the adults in their life care about their well-being and safety. These feelings of security fill the child with a sense of security and self-confidence.

During the early years, a child's self-esteem is formed by the adults and family members around him. He will, at an early age, gain an understanding of the qualities and attributes that are considered important in a family. For instance, if a child comes from a very athletic family, but is rather clumsy or awkward, he may start to feel bad about himself. If a child comes from a family group that values high intellect, and he has trouble learning, he may stumble with his self-esteem. If the grown-ups who are important to him are sensitive to this and focus on the child's strengths, his self-esteem will recover.

It is important that parents and teachers—who are possibly the most influential adults that a child knows—are always aware of the ramifications of their words and actions on a child's self-esteem.

As a child grows older, his teachers and peers begin to have an affect on his self-esteem. Because this year's child is becoming more aware of his surroundings socially, he may struggle with his self-esteem. He will become aware of the qualities and attributes that his peers value, and will artificially come to value those same qualities. He is becoming more aware of his looks, abilities, and intellect, and how it relates to the other members of his peer group.

Similarly, if your third grader has older siblings who succeed in a given subject or field, he may feel extra pressure to live up to the legacy left behind by his sibling. As parents, we must hone in on the qualities that make this child special. Comparing a younger child to an older sibling only creates more pressure on an already fragile and budding self-esteem.

How to Nurture Self-Esteem

As they grow, children become increasingly sensitive to the evaluations of their peers. You and your child's teachers can help your child learn to build healthy relationships with his or her peers.

When children develop stronger ties with their peers in school or around the neighborhood, they may begin to evaluate themselves differently. Your child will begin to form his own opinion of where he fits in with friends and family members by noticing values and qualities of those around him. You can help your child by being clear about your own values and keeping the lines of communication open about experiences outside the home.

Children do not acquire self-esteem at once nor do they always feel good about themselves in every situation. A child may feel self-confident and accepted at home but not around the neighborhood or in school. Furthermore, as children interact with their peers or learn to function in school or some other place, they may feel accepted and liked one moment and feel different the next. Because you are still the most important person in your third grader's life, you can help by giving consistent and honest reassurance to your child. Your approval, appreciation, and admiration will balance the scales of self-esteem.

If you find your child despondent and full of self-doubt, consider offering him inspirational stories of triumph. Biographies of Albert Einstein or Helen Keller are a great place to start. Perhaps someone in your own family overcame a problem before succeeding. Share with him so that he knows his happiness can come from within.

GREAT IDEA!

A child's sense of self-worth is more likely to deepen when adults respond to the child's interests and efforts with appreciation rather than just praise. For example, if your child shows interest in something you are doing, you might include the child in the activity. Or if the child shows interest in an animal in the garden, you might help the child find more information about it. In this way, you respond positively to your child's interest by treating it seriously. Flattery and praise, on the contrary, distract children from the topics they are interested in. Children may develop a habit of showing interest in a topic just to receive flattery.

Self-esteem is most likely to be fostered when children are esteemed by the adults who are important to them. To esteem children means to treat them respectfully, ask their views and opinions, take their views and opinions seriously, and give them meaningful and realistic feedback.

You can help your child develop and maintain healthy self-esteem by helping him or her cope with defeats, rather than emphasizing constant successes and triumphs. During times of disappointment or crisis, your child's weakened self-esteem can be strengthened when you let the child know that your love and support remain unchanged. When the crisis has passed, you can help your child reflect on what went wrong. The next time a crisis occurs, your child can use the knowledge gained from overcoming past difficulties to help cope with a new crisis. A child's sense of self-worth and self-confidence is not likely to deepen when adults deny that life has its ups and downs.

FINDING HIS PLACE

THROUGHOUT kindergarten, first, and second grades, children tend to play together in groups. They are one class, one group, one mission. They play group games well with little thought of each other's talents. They work together on projects with little regard to which student is the "smartest" or the "most popular." Learning and playing are fun games, and the entire class is a team working toward one goal, with the teacher perceived as a coach, of sorts.

Third-grade children are different. This year is very much about socializing, learning one's place in a group, and how to relate to others. While the third-grade child is still a team player, he prefers to choose his own team. He will begin to choose his peer group, his friends. He may see one of his peers, or even himself, in the position of "coach," the position formerly held by a teacher.

Your child is making his own niche in third grade. He will choose his friends instead of arbitrarily playing with the classmate closest to the seesaw at recess. During recess and other recreational activities, a certain pecking order will begin to sort itself out. While running, jumping, and playing, leaders take command of the play and followers quickly heed their chosen leader's instructions, whether those instructions are spoken or merely implied. Your third grader may play on the jungle gym every day during lunch recess simply because his team chooses to play there.

Usually this follower/leader behavior is not unhealthy. Just because your child is a follower does not mean that she is being bullied into that role. Perhaps being a follower on the team is a more comfortable proposition for her than leading the way. There is no need to be disappointed with your third grader for not being the leader, and she should not be pressured into thinking that she has to be the leader.

Children of this age are "labelers." Similar to the names of positions played by members of a baseball team, these labels are used to describe members of your third grader's team. Your third grader will tend to notice his peers, the adults in his life, and the relationships between them. He will use labels and phrases to describe how he feels about that person, or how that person fits into his team. You will hear your third grader say things like, "Jessica is the best reader!" or "Kyle runs very fast!" when referring to classmates and friends. He will use these same labels when describing himself. Upon meeting someone for the first time, your third grader may blurt out matter-of-factly, "I read chapter books now!" When conveying his feelings about relationships, your third grader may utter such comments as, "Mrs. Smith likes Tommy the best" or "Jill is the teacher's pet." He may also make less kind remarks like, "I don't like him, he is not good at kickball!"

These statements are not always true; they are the perception of your child as he relates to the world around him. Take note to your third grader's tone of voice when he makes these comments to you. Is he envious, concerned, dejected, or happy to see his friend succeed? Are his comments indicative of his current self-esteem level? Is your third grader saying these things because it is what his friends say? Is he only echoing the thoughts of others? Is he fighting some self-esteem issues that are causing him to be negative when relating to others? Be in tune to what your child is saying, and what he isn't saying. His inflections, tones, and omissions often speak louder than the words he utters. These statements could be products of low self-esteem, honest reaction, or of a new force—peer pressure.

PEER PRESSURE AND ACCEPTANCE

DURING the previous school years, your child was concerned with gaining the approval and appreciation of the adults in her life—her teacher and adult family members. She would do almost anything for those adults in her life that she valued. Because her peer group was at the same general social and emotional level, her actions were not noticed or judged by her classmates. Now that the entire class has grown physically and emotionally, they are noticing each other more and more. Children with high self-esteem will often become the leaders and will become the figures that other children will want to emulate. The third-grade child will not only want to emulate those in their class who are more popular or who are leaders, but they will feel pressure from other classmates to conform to the behavioral or social standards of the popular majority.

Friendships become more important this year as children begin to show their individuality in the way they dress, music they like, and through recreational interests. Although your child probably has had many friendships since beginning school in kindergarten, this years friendships are a bit different. Your child may have a best friend this year instead of the pool of many best friends common in the earlier grades.

Your child's new knowledge of government and civics is put to the test as clubs and cliques are formed. You may hear a group of third graders discussing their plans for their new group, including who will be the leader, what the rule will be for entry in the group, and who will and who will not be allowed to join. For instance, in the classic television show, *The Little Rascals*, the boys in the club had a rule, "No Girls Allowed." Do not be surprised to find that your child's group of friends has formed a club or clique with it's own similar set of rules, whether they are formal or unspoken.

Although the term "peer pressure" often makes us think negatively, it is important that we realize that there are two types of peer pressure, good and bad. Some peer pressure is very positive and encourages our children to work hard, be good citizens, and to excel. Admittedly there are also negative peer pressure forces that can cause our children to feel stressed into making poor decisions.

An example of negative peer pressure is displayed in the following anecdote:

Julie and Cindy were on the playground. Julie had a ball that she was kicking and throwing with some of her friends. When Cindy came up and asked to join the fun, Julie responded, "No! Go away. You cannot play with us because you wear glasses." Cindy's face became very sad, she dropped her head, slumped a bit, and began to walk away. One of Julie's friends in the group chimed in with the chant, "Four-eyes, four-eyes . . . " As several others in the group started singing along with the chant, another girl in the group, Sally, felt very torn between helping Cindy, and joining the chants of the group. Eventually she started singing along with the others in the group, "four-eyes, four-eyes . . . " Sally knew that this was not good behavior, but wanted to fit in with her friends, so she continued the chant although Cindy's feelings were hurt.

An example of positive peer pressure in the same situation is displayed here:

Julie and Cindy were on the playground. Julie had a ball that she was kicking and throwing with some of her friends. When Cindy came up and asked to join the fun, Julie responded, "No! Go away. You cannot play with us because you wear glasses." Cindy's face became very sad, she dropped her head, slumped a bit, and began to walk away. Suddenly one of the other girls playing ball, Sally, ran over to Cindy. "Sure Cindy, you can play with us, come on," she said to the sad little girl. Other girls who were playing ball also encouraged Cindy to join the game. Sally looked at Julie and exclaimed, "Cindy is going to play with us, too. You should apologize." Suddenly Julie felt very foolish for her uncaring remark and promptly apologized. The group of girls played together the rest of the recess and all got along just fine.

In the example of negative peer pressure, Sally allowed herself to be influenced by what the rest of the girls were doing. She felt pressure by her peers to behave in a way that she knew was not acceptable. In the example of positive peer pressure, Sally and the other girls took the lead, and set the stage for the acceptable behavior on the playground. The reactions and remarks of Sally and her friend weighed upon Julie and made her rethink her behavior. She realized that in order to be part of the group, she was going to have to behave in an appropriate manner.

Children with good self-esteem are better prepared and equipped to make the right decisions in situations where peer pressure is evident. Praising and commending a child for making the right decisions contributes to the child's feelings of self-worth and will encourage a child to continue to make good decisions.

We all long for our children to be accepted by their friends and classmates. Acceptance by one's peers has far-reaching implications. Studies now show that being accepted by and involved with your peer group at a young age directly affects one's abilities to interact with others as adolescents and young adults. Being accepted and approved of in a group of one's peers allows for your child to be involved in many social activities. In this case practice makes perfect. Involvement in social activities allows your child to build upon their social skills, learn new social skills, and gives them a feeling of self-worth. This helps build their level of self-esteem.

There are several factors that can affect a child's acceptance by his peers. These may include:

➤ **Social Behavior**—A child who is not well behaved may be outcast by his peers. Also, a child who is extremely introverted may not allow himself the opportunity to be accepted.

➤ **Difference**—Almost any physical or social feature that makes a child stand out, such as handicap, intellectual growth, or ethnic background, can cause difficulty in relating to peers.

➤ **Family Problems**—The child who is experiencing family upheaval such as a divorce or recent death of a loved one may act out in school and around friends, or may become reluctant to make friends.

➤ **Reputation**—Although a child may not have social problems now, if he is "known" (whether real or imagined) to have a social problem, whether alcoholic parent, poor behavior, or extreme shyness, he may have trouble getting past the reputation to social acceptance.

COOTIES AND OTHER CREATURES

HARD to believe as it is, your third grader is beginning to notice that there are third graders of the opposite sex. This does not mean that your third grader is going to be involved in a typical girlfriend/boyfriend type of relationship. Instead of the more mature girlfriend/boyfriend relationship, your third grader will have other ways of showing interest in the opposite sex. A third grader will often show negative attention to the object of their affection. His favorite girl in the class may suddenly "have cooties" or become his favorite target for jokes and games. Her favorite boy in the class may be coerced into chasing her and her friends on the playground at recess. Occasionally two third graders will find themselves in "like" and will openly admit their mutual attraction to one another, their peers, and family members. These infatuations are harmless and indicative of normal, healthy self-esteem and social growth.

TOLERANCE

NOW that our children are getting older, and more aware of the world around them, they may start noticing physical, religious, or ethnical differences in their friends and classmates. In today's global environment, it is probable that your child will interact with children of different races, colors, abilities, and religions. Children most often mimic the attitudes of their parents and family members, therefore you should be careful to promote an environment of tolerance and understanding.

Your third grader will be proud of his heritage. Because he is also filled with the sense that he must always be right, he may be quick to judge others on their differences. When your child comes to you with questions about why a friend is a different color than they are, or why they celebrate a different holiday, be sure to give accurate answers. If you don't know the answers, you may want to plan a small research project for the two of you. Your tolerant and non-prejudice behavior will speak volumes to your child.

SCHOOL VIOLENCE

OUR children are growing up in a more violent and threatening world, and it is rearing it's ugly head even within our educational institutions. School violence has several levels of severity. In the past the most common and most severe school violence was the type of fear and intimidation emanated by a school bully. Unfortunately, in this age of guns, gangs, and a brief but tragic history of school violence, we now have to include much more severe forms of school violence when discussing third grade.

Bullies

Certain direct behaviors—such as teasing, taunting, threatening, hitting, and stealing that are initiated by one or more students against a victim—are considered to be bullying. In addition to direct attacks, bullying may also occur using more insidious methods—such as spreading rumors about someone to cause them to become socially isolated. While boys typically engage in direct bullying methods, girls who bully are more apt to utilize these more subtle, indirect strategies. By the time a child completes their educational career, there is a 15 percent chance that they will have been victimized by a bully. Bullying tends to start in elementary school, with a steady rise in occurrence until it peaks in middle school.

A child who bullies others, contrary to myths, tends to have very high self-esteem, and may be a physically superior child. The bully yearns to have power and control over others, and turns to socially inappropriate tactics to make this yearning a reality. Often times a bully comes from a background where physical strength and prowess are used to control one's surroundings and solve problems. Even parents who work hard to raise healthy well-adjusted children will occasionally find out that their child has been inflicting some sort of control over another person. Do not allow yourself to feel like a failure. Instead, try to constructively work through this difficult time.

If you suspect that your child is a bully:

➤ Do not give them a taste of their own medicine. All you will be doing is encouraging the idea that it is alright to inflict pain on another person.

➤ Although you may be angry and upset, it would be more worthwhile to sit the child down and talk about it, explaining that it is cruel to hurt another person whether physically or mentally.

➤ Ask them to imagine what it must feel like to be on the receiving end.

➤ Make sure they know that you will not tolerate bullying.

➤ Ask them to think of a way they can make amends with the victim. Offer solutions, such as apologizing, but also encourage your child to think of ways to resolve this situation.

➤ Keep in touch with your child's teacher and ask to be kept informed about your child's behavior and whether the bullying has stopped.

➤ When your child does stop bullying let them know that you are pleased with them.

➤ Ask yourself why your child has reached the stage where they have had to bully another child.

The child who is victimized is often physically weaker than the aggressor. Other physical characteristics such as weight, dress, or wearing eyeglasses do not appear to be contributing factors leading to victimization. Typically, students who are victims of bullying are anxious, insecure, cautious, and suffer from low self-esteem. They rarely will be found defending themselves or retaliating when confronted by students who bully them. Often times they are children who are very close to their parents, sometimes to the point that the parents are described as being overprotective. For this reason, bullies often rationalize their own behavior by proclaiming that they are "toughening up" their victim.

A bullied child may:

➤ be frightened of walking to or from school, so much so that they will change the usual route, not want to go on the school bus, or beg you to drive them to school.

➤ be unwilling to go outdoors to play.

➤ feel ill in the mornings.

➤ begin skipping school.

➤ begin doing poorly in their school work.

➤ come home regularly with clothes or books destroyed.

➤ come home hungry (bully has stolen lunch, or lunch money).

➤ become withdrawn.

➤ start stammering.

➤ lack confidence.

➤ become distressed and anxious.

➤ cry themselves to sleep.

➤ suddenly begin to lose possessions and/or money, such as allowance.

➤ ask for money or start stealing money (to pay bully).

➤ have unexplained scratches, bruises, cuts.

➤ begin to bully other children themselves.

➤ become aggressive and unreasonable.

➤ give improbable excuses to explain any of the above.

If you suspect that your child is being bullied:

➤ Listen to your child and find out if others are not treating your child as they should. This will encourage your child to trust you and come to you when there is a problem.

➤ Help your child consider various ways of dealing with a particular problem.

➤ If the problem is the way another child is behaving, suggest working out the problem by talking with the other child, or a responsible adult.

➤ If the problem is another adult, however, or if your child is seriously threatened by other children, you will need to intervene directly.

STRATEGIES TO BEAT SCHOOL VIOLENCE

SCHOOLS and communities are banding together to promote a safer, more amicable environment for the children and citizens of their communities. Some of the techniques include:

➤ *Teaching prevention skills.* Students are being taught mediation skills (problem solving and communication) and ways to handle their emotions—especially anger—without hurting others. These skills will help them avoid potentially dangerous situations. Students are also being taught "safe" behaviors such as doing activities in groups, alerting school personnel if a stranger is on school grounds, and reporting situations that threaten other students' safety.

➤ *Providing alternatives to gangs.* School districts and communities are working together to offer students alternatives to gang membership, including activities that build self-esteem and help students deal with feelings of powerlessness. Strategies include providing special assistance to students who are at risk of gang membership, creating an atmosphere that fosters a sense of belonging in all students, informing parents and school staff about gangs and teaching students how to avoid being drawn into them, and giving students regular opportunities to discuss school experiences and to plan for future successes and rewards.

➤ *Improving school designs.* As new school buildings are constructed and old ones are renovated, safety has become an essential element of their design. In new schools, office areas are now centrally located for easy accessibility from other locations in the building or campus. Hallways have convenient exits and are well lit. Dead-end hallways and staircase hideaways have been eliminated, and restrooms are located closer to administrators to prevent students from hanging out.

➤ *Monitoring visitors carefully.* Schools are becoming more assertive in screening visitors, requiring them to register when entering the building or campus and by employing security personnel. Schools can be both secure and friendly by requesting visitors to check in rather than report to the office. Registered visitors are given a pass or badge to display prominently to let staff and students know that they have been acknowledged by the administration. Staff and students are instructed to report people without proper identification to a school administrator. In addition, many schools now ask that parents give the names of adults who are allowed to pick up a child, and require those individuals to show identification to school personnel when signing a student out.

HOW CAN I HELP MY CHILD PRACTICE SAFE BEHAVIOR?

PARENTS can teach their children safe behaviors before enrolling them in school. Children who know the appropriate action to take in a given situation are less likely to expose themselves to danger. Safe behaviors to teach your child are some of the same lessons taught to us by our parents. They include:

➤ *Not talking to strangers.* This warning is more important today than ever before. Encourage your children to get to know school staff other than their teachers and get acquainted with them yourself. Familiarity helps children recognize adults who don't belong as well as adults who can offer help when needed. As a plus, children will also learn that the school staff are their friends and more than just rule enforcers.

➤ *Taking safety in numbers.* Encourage your children to stay close to friends and to walk in groups in school hallways. Suggest that they limit their restroom visits to recess and breaks and use facilities located in high-traffic areas or in areas more likely to be visited by staff.

➤ *Choosing friends carefully.* Encourage your children to avoid students who do not handle anger effectively. Ask your children to be particularly careful with classmates who bring weapons to school and to report any such incidents to their teachers.

As a parent, make it your responsibility to become as active in your child's education as your schedule permits. In addition to some of the parental involvement tips provided in Chapter 1, here are some strategies you can use:

> *Visit school frequently*, being sure to register with administrative personnel when you arrive. Volunteer to help in your child's classroom or elsewhere in the school as often as you can and encourage other parents to visit and volunteer. The more parents are involved and visible, the safer their children's schools will be.

> *Become a member of the Parent-Teacher Association (PTA)* or other parent-teacher organization. By attending meetings and participating in its committees and activities, you'll become acquainted with other parents and with school personnel.

> *Get to know your child's friends and their families.* Productive friendships and a sense of common purpose among students, teachers, and neighbors make schools and neighborhoods safer.

While critics state that the Internet is unsafe for children, there are in fact a number of sites where parents and children can learn about safety.

■ www.usfa.fema.gov/kids/ The United States Fire Administration has created this site specifically for children to teach them about preventing fires and escaping them. Games and graphics make learning about fire safety fun, not scary.

■ www.fema.gov/kids/ready.htm The purpose of this site is to help children to prepare for disasters. FEMA (Federal Emergency Management Agency) uses cartoon characters to teach children many valuable lessons about disaster preparedness.

■ ww.fda.gov/oc/opacom/kids/default.htm The Food and Drug Administration has created a site complete with games and quizzes to teach children about everything from food safety to preventing tobacco usage.

■ www.cpssc.gov/kids/kidsafety/main1.html Even the Consumer Product Safety Commission has a site to teach children how to reduce the risk of injury related to consumer products. Kidd, a friendly goat, leads children through games about safety.

WRAPPING IT UP

WITH all the new pressures of third grade, it is important that you are prepared for the emotional and social explosion that your child will be experiencing. Your third grader will be quick to laugh, quick to cry, walk tall, become timid, all within a short period of time. Be aware that your child's emotional and social growth can span more than two years. This means that your third grader may have the conversational skills of a nine-year-old, but the self-confidence of a seven-year-old. In other aspects of his social growth, your third grader may be right on track.

The phrase, "the apple doesn't fall far from the tree" is often too true when we discuss our children. For this reason, it is important that parents are good role models to their children. In almost every aspect of life—racial and religious tolerance, bullying, organizational skills, and social interaction—children will emulate the behavior they have witnessed in their caregivers.

Finally, each child is gloriously different. Remember to be in tune with your child's needs, skills, and abilities. You are perhaps the best barometer of your third grader's social growth. Try not to gauge your child comparatively to the other children in his grade, but to his previous social skills. As long as his skills are advancing and not regressing, he is probably doing just fine.

If your child shows any serious emotional or social growth issues, please contact a professional. Your school counselor, family pediatrician, or other healthcare professional can help you explore your child's difficulties, offer solutions and treatment methods, and give you peace of mind.

5

The 3rd Grade Partnership: You, Your Child, Your Child's Teacher

OFTEN when it comes to children, each adult involved with that child is sure that they hold the best knowledge, opinions, and solutions that will ensure that child's success. This behavior is first noted in adults at the birth of a new baby. From the time the umbilical cord is cut, there are adults—grandparents, aunts, uncles, sisters, cousins, neighbors, friends—who are sure that their ideas for nurturing and caring for a child are the only correct ways to care for a child—and they are not shy about sharing their ideas. With time, parents are able to understand that these advisors are not trying to interfere, but trying to help them raise the best person they can. They learn to filter out extraneous information, and as parents, maintain the balance that is right for their child.

When faced with the education of their children, parents must become comfortable in sharing the responsibility with other adults. All members of the educational team must treat one another with respect and courtesy. Open-mindedness is important.

Both the parent and the teacher see the child in different circumstances, surroundings, and with different groups of children. For this reason, the parent and the teacher may observe opposing patterns of behavior in the same child. Many parents find themselves uncomfortable knowing that another adult in their child's life has taken on the role of advisor, teacher, and disciplinarian, even if only for six hours a day. Occasionally parents and teachers will find themselves in a power struggle, each exasperated with the behavior and actions of the other. I have heard of teachers who have received visits from disgruntled parents at home, after school hours. Also, I have been made aware of teachers who have been so rude to parents during open house events that the parents were left speechless. Neither of these courses of action is conducive to a good learning environment for your child. It is imperative that parents and teachers are able to forge an agreement that is focused on one goal—the child's educational success.

"I have tried to keep the communication between my daughter's teacher and myself open. I work full time outside the home, so it is difficult to be at school often, however, I never missed an open house or a parent-teacher conference. I go on at least one field trip each year, and attended all her pageants, etc. This year my daughter's teacher and I write a lot of notes back and forth so even though I'm not in the classroom very often, I carry on a continuing dialog with her regarding my daughter. Because of the continuing communication with the teacher, I understand that this teacher really has keen insight into my child. She is a good source of information and advice."

—A Parent from California

It is to the best advantage of your child that the educational experience be as smooth and dispute-free as possible. In order for this to happen, you, your child, and your child's teacher must work together as a team. If all three of the team members accept their role on the team, and are willing to work toward the same goals, then success is almost always guaranteed. Each team member has roles and responsibilities on the team. It is important that each member knows these responsibilities and is willing to do their part to ensure the success of the team.

Responsibilities of the Parent

Children of involved parents tend to have better grades, a more positive school attitude, and behave more appropriately at school than their peers with uninvolved parents. For that reason it is imperative that you, the parent, do not underestimate your roll on your child's educational team, regardless of your own education. Although the parent's attitude and involvement are extremely important to the success of the child, the parent sometimes feels the most disjointed of the team members. Because the parent is not present during most of the school day, it is easy to become uninvolved in the educational experience. Don't let this happen to you.

Often, parents do not involve themselves in their child's education unless something negative occurs. This is called "reactive parenting." The parent reacts to a bad grade, a disciplinary concern, or other school related problem. Frequently, this reaction is not positive, nor is it especially productive. In many occasions, the reactive parent has not visited the school, has not attended open house events, nor parent-teacher conferences. If the reactive parent's first visit to the teacher is in a reactionary mode, the visit is destined to be a tense and uneasy meeting. The angry, upset, or disillusioned reactive parent may find that their already high emotional level may be exacerbated by the unfamiliar surroundings of the school.

Another type of parenting is "proactive parenting." The proactive parent prepares and plans for the child's educational experience. The proactive parent takes on responsibilities as a team member immediately. This parent knows who their child's teacher is, feels comfortable contacting this teacher, and knows where their child's classroom is in a school. This parent may take time to:

➤ Visit their child's classroom; a visit will give an idea of what your child does at school and how he or she interacts with other children.

➤ Volunteer to help in the classroom as an assistant (listening to children read, for example, or serving as an aide during computer work).

➤ Support student events and performances by helping with them (such as sewing costumes or painting scenery for a school play) and by attending them.

➤ If the school has a Parents' Room/Lounge or Parent Center, drop in to meet other parents and teachers there, or to pick up information and materials.

➤ Participate in workshops that are offered, such as those on child development or concerns that parents have (or help plan such workshops).

Take advantage of parent-teacher contracts (example: to read with your child for a certain amount of time each night). If no such contract exists, talk to school administrators about starting one. Share this concept with other concerned parents. It will reinforce the commitment that both you and the teacher are making.

➤ Ask your child's teacher if he or she has materials that can be used to help your child at home and to supplement homework.

➤ Be part of decision-making committees about school issues and problems, such as a Parent Advisory Committee.

➤ Attend parent-teacher conferences and other opportunities for parent-teacher interaction.

You may also want to refer to Chapter 1 for more discussion on parental involvement in a child's education.

If a proactive parent is summoned to the school to deal with disciplinary or academic issues, they will probably walk into the school with an air of confidence. They will already be comfortable checking in at the school office, walking to the meeting room, or classroom, greeting the teacher, and will be ready for the topic of discussion. This comfort level allows for even a difficult conference to have an aura of productivity, rather than the pallor of confrontation. Parent–teacher conflicts are discussed later in this chapter.

As mentioned, studies have shown that parental involvement in a child's education is effective in ensuring a child's success—regardless of the family's financial or educational background. This means that parental involvement is not just for the rich, nor is it only for the educated. Therefore, all parents, by definition, have the tools to ensure that their child is a successful student. At home you, as a parent, can:

➤ Have high expectations for your child's learning and behavior, both at home and at school.

➤ Praise and encourage your child.

➤ Emphasize effort and achievement, and be a role model for getting work done before play.

➤ Establish rules and routines in the home.

➤ Monitor television viewing, video game playtime, and computer usage.

➤ Limit after-school activities.

➤ Encourage your child to share information about school and respond with empathy.

➤ If you don't do anything else, read to your young child or have him or her read to you every night. Encourage older children to read, by reading yourself and by having interesting and appropriate materials available.

Teacher Point of View

Recently a group of parents gathered together for a discussion on the parent/teacher/child relationship. Among the group of parents was one woman who happened to be a teacher. She observed and processed the conversation at hand, then offered her insights not only as a parent, but also as a teaching professional. She supplied the parents at the discussion with a list of facts of which teachers would like parents to be aware.

➤ We are professionals. We have the best interest of your children at heart. If a parent has a problem with me, I would prefer that he/she comes to me first and give me a chance to explain/find out what's happening directly, rather than being blindsided or hearing it from another teacher or parent or my principal. Parents are encouraged to make an appointment to see me so I can be prepared with your child's information and we can discuss it.

➤ Unlike other professionals, we deal with 20 to 25 students at a time. If a teacher approaches you with an issue, most of the time, it comes from a genuine concern for your child. Teachers work very hard to manage, get to know, support, and challenge each student individually. And don't forget other "unofficial" responsibilities: This includes everyone's lunch money, jewelry that falls off, as well as what each child is saying and doing to each other child all day long.

➤ Don't let a little problem get to be a big one before helping me solve it. If I request a conference with a parent, it is to brainstorm with you and get ideas as to how to best help your child have maximum success in my classroom, or how to solve a problem before it escalates.

➤ Let your child be as responsible for his things as he can. If you constantly cover for him (for example, always bring forgotten items, always make excuses for his grades or behavior, always take your child's word without giving me a chance or believing what I say) this will give the child the message that it's PARENT against TEACHER instead of us working as a team. In this situation, no one wins—least of all your child.

➤ Help your child to arrive at school on time. If she's always late, she's missing a lot. If she's not there, I can't teach her. Particularly in the lower grades, so much of the daily lesson is based upon class participation that really cannot be made up alone, later on.

The same parent/teacher then commented as a mother, and not as a teacher. Here is the credo of an involved parent:

➤ I am the only advocate that my child has. If I have a problem/question with someone/something at school, it is my obligation to my child to find out how I can help them solve it.

➤ I want to be involved in my child's education. I believe that education begins at home. I work but make sure that I am at the school when I can. I attend some PTA meetings, always go to open house, and try to take at least one afternoon off to make at least one party or field trip during the year.

> If your child seems unhappy with school, or has a bad attitude, regardless of your level of involvement, it is time for you to use your parental instincts to help find the cause of your child's sadness. Using your unique insight into your child, try to find out why he or she seems unhappy with school. Observe and listen to your child. The problem may not lie with school itself, but with peers or friends. It may also be a family problem or an issue of self-esteem. Arrange for a conference with the teacher or school counselor. Work toward being able to discuss problems with your child openly, and listen carefully to his or her views before you offer any solutions.

> ➤ I am on a team with the teacher. My child will always see us as a unified front working for the best interest of her. If I have a conflict with you, the teacher, I will schedule a conference with you without my child present to discuss the matter first. Then, if needed, I will talk with you along with my child. You are my child's boss at school, I demand that she respect you, just as I expect her to respect me at home. I will treat the teacher with respect because you are a professional.

THE TEACHER

THE teacher is also a part of the team, a very important part of the team. Many parents can look back at their school career and name the one teacher who somehow touched them. Perhaps there was something about one of your teachers that was memorable—maybe a quick smile, the way she taught math that was easy to understand, or the effortless way she earned the respect of the students. For whatever reason, this teacher made an impact on your life. We often measure our children's teachers against the memory of this teacher. Keep in mind that all teachers and all students have different teaching and learning styles. Your child may thrive under an excellent teacher whose methodologies may be very unfamiliar to you. This is often the case, and rest assured, your child will learn what he needs to in this important year.

Over the past few years, your child's teachers may have filled the role of daycare provider, mother, and even sometimes playmate. This year will be a bit different. Your child's teacher will still be an integral part of your child's life, but you will find that she will not coddle your child as much as years prior to third grade. This year your child's teacher will expect her to take responsibility for homework and other school responsibilities, such as lunch money and the return of permission slips.

Many parents have predisposed ideas about a teacher prior to their child becoming a student in that teacher's classroom. These predisposed opinions may originate from conversation with other parents, a bad first impression, or from fears that may be expressed by children. It is not uncommon for a child to say, "I hope that Mrs. Brown is not my teacher. She gives a lot of homework!" While some of these statements may be true, and networking with other parents is a valuable way to gain information about your school system, the administrators, and the teachers to whom you are entrusting your children, the responsible parent should keep an open mind and allow their own experiences to drive their opinions. It is imperative that parents respect the teacher, and do not allow their personal views of the teacher taint their child's experience.

A responsible, team-oriented teacher will supply opportunities for even the timid parent to become involved. Some of the strategies that your child's teacher may employ are:

> **Let parents know how and when they can contact the school and the teacher.** Early in the school year, teachers can explain that they can be reached at specific times or in specific ways; can be contacted directly as questions or concerns arise; and have given a lot of thought to their teaching philosophies, class rules, and expectations. In addition to personal interaction, teachers can use newsletters or can send letters home to provide this information to parents.

> **Elicit expressions of parents' concerns and interests in preparation for parent–teacher conferences.** Early in the school year, ask parents to share their main concerns and goals for their child. Brief questionnaires and interest surveys also provide good bases for meaningful discussions in parent–teacher conferences

> **Practice an open-door, open-mind policy.** Teachers can invite parents to visit the classroom at any time that is convenient to the parents. When they visit, parents can monitor their child's perceptions of a situation and can see for themselves what the teacher is trying to achieve with his or her students.

> **Involve parents in classroom activities.** Teachers can let parents know how they can be helpful and can solicit their assistance with specific activities. The more involved parents are in what goes on in the classroom, the more likely they are to understand the teacher's goals and practices.

SHOULD I REQUEST MY CHILD'S TEACHER?

I N many schools across the nation, the practice of requesting a child's teacher for the next year has become common. The practice, if you are unfamiliar, allows parents to contact the school at the end of one school year to express their preferences for their child's teacher for the following year. While some schools embrace teacher requests, this practice has become a hot topic among parents and administrators.

Some schools have disallowed the practice of teacher requesting because then it becomes an abused tool. Other schools openly encourage parents to express their wishes, and even publicize the deadlines for teacher requests.

Proponents of teacher requesting say that requesting their child's teacher:

> is a form of parental involvement.
> ensures that a child is placed with a teacher fitting his personality.
> is necessary, because most parents are doing it.

Opponents of the same practice believe that teacher requests:

> often mean that the children of the uninvolved parents, who are often the neediest students, get a teacher who is not a good match for them.
> are often based on parental emotions than actual facts.
> only cause unnecessary work for our teachers and administrators.

The mediocre teacher tells. The good teacher explains. The superior teacher demonstrates. The great teacher inspires.

—WILLIAM A. WARD, EDUCATOR

If you have genuine concerns about your child's learning style, and have observed that she thrives in a particular type of environment, you may want to consider requesting a certain type of learning environment, rather than a particular teacher. Also, if you have concerns about your child's teacher and classroom for the next year, have a frank discussion with your child's teacher this year. Chances are that your child's current teacher, administrators, and counselors will be more than happy to listen to your concerns.

You need a perfect mix of personality to achieve the highest level of learning. As a parent and a teacher, I think it is great if you have the opportunity to choose your child's teacher. You may know that your child's structured work habits may not go with a care-free teacher's work environment; or that your child has a creative style and the teacher is not inclined that way. I am not saying that we should put our students in a class just because the teacher has made some great accomplishment or that everyone likes him/her better than another teacher. I think that when you are choosing your child's teacher based on which teacher is "better" (according to everyone else's standards) you are making a mistake. Examine how well your child will work with any given teacher and evaluate the situation accordingly.

— A PARENT OF A THIRD GRADER, WHO ALSO HAPPENS TO BE
A TEACHER, NEW YORK

PARENT-TEACHER CONFERENCES

PARENT-TEACHER conferences are a great way to meet your child's teacher. This is one of the prime occasions that you will have to get to know your child's teacher and discuss your child's progress. Do not be intimidated by your child's teacher; remember you are both on the same team, with your child's best interest at heart. You will find that having a respectful, open relationship with your child's teacher alleviates stress that your child may feel at school and fostering a good rapport will give you peace of mind in knowing that your child's needs are being met.

Even if you are aware of no problems with your child, academically or behavioral, you should attend these conferences. The parent-teacher conference provides opportunity to interact with the teacher without children present. While you may have an open stream of communication with your child's teacher, the conference will afford you the occasion to have a valuable, and frank discussion with your teammate in your child's educational training.

ADDRESSING ACADEMIC PROBLEMS

ALMOST every child will, at some time in her educational career, experience some level of academic difficulty. This is one of the common topics discussed at a parent-teacher conference. The United States Department of Education offers some strategies that have proven to be useful when discussing a child's learning problems with the teacher.

> ➤ **Consider the context of the problem.** Ask the teacher to be specific about the problem and the context in which the problem occurs. Children who experience difficulty in learning may do so for many reasons. They may be experiencing frustrations with peers, with family arrangements, or with specific subjects or learning situations. It may be beneficial for teachers to pinpoint both strengths and weaknesses that the child displays. Parents can then work with teachers to identify specific situations in which the difficulty occurs.
>
> ➤ **Identify successful strategies.** Ask the teacher what is being done to help the child overcome the problem. Ideally, the teacher has tried several strategies to help the child overcome the learning problem. Sometimes small steps, such as moving a child to a different place in the room or shortening an assignment, can make a difference. Often children find it difficult to let the teacher know that they do not understand what is expected of them. It may be helpful to have the teacher talk to the child about his or her problem along with the parent.
>
> ➤ **Make a plan.** Ask the teacher what you can specifically do to help the child at home. With the teacher, list three or four concrete actions to do every day. It may be as simple as a change in the evening schedule so that the child has 15 to 20 minutes of the parent's time to read together or work on math homework. A regular schedule is usually beneficial to a child. A young child might benefit from two shorter periods of work rather than one long session. For example, it may be more effective to learn to spell three new words a night than to study 10 or 12 words the night before a test.
>
> ➤ **Arrange for follow up communications.** Before leaving the conference, it is a good idea to agree with the teacher on what is expected of

the child, what the teacher will do to help, and what the parent will do. Sometimes it is helpful to involve the child in these decisions so that she can see that the teacher and parents are working together to help alleviate the problem. A follow-up conference can be used to review the effectiveness of the plan and to formulate a new plan, if necessary. Scheduling another meeting after three to four weeks signals to the child that both parents and teachers are highly interested in taking effective steps to help her achieve success in learning. This strategy can serve to encourage a child who may have become discouraged from repeated experiences of failure early in the school year.

ADDRESSING BEHAVIOR PROBLEMS

SOME of the more difficult problems to address at school are behavioral issues. Many children will, at some time, act out and get in trouble in school. Because third grade is a year of immense social growth, even a model student may experience brief bouts of behavior problems in third grade. Usually repeated misbehavior, or an unusual change in a child's behavior pattern will result in a conference between the parent and teacher. It is important that all team members attend this meeting with open minds, and with one focus—to solve the problem that is causing the child to act out. Some of important conference tactics include:

➤ **Specify the behavior.** Ask the teacher to be specific about the type of misbehavior in which the child engages. Aggressive behavior may be a child's way of getting something from a peer rather than of intentionally bringing harm to another person. Inability to follow directions may be a result of a hearing or language problem rather than evidence of direct defiance of the teacher. It is helpful to consider many possibilities when pinpointing the behavior in question.

➤ **Examine the context.** Ask the teacher to help determine when, where, and why the misbehavior is occurring. Try to identify with the teacher any events that may have contributed to a specific incident of misconduct. Try to take into consideration anything that might be contributing to the situation: the influence of peers, time of day, family problems, illness or fatigue, or changes in schedule or after-school activities. Children may be more prone to misconduct when they are tired or irritable.

➤ **Examine the teacher's expectations.** Ask the teacher to be as specific as possible about what a child does that is different from what the teacher expects in a particular situation. Sometimes, if the teacher assumes that a child is being intentionally aggressive, the teacher's expectation of aggressive acts can become part of the problem and can lead to a "recursive cycle" in which children come to fulfill the expectations set for them. Try to determine with the teacher if the child is capable of meeting the teacher's positive expectations.

➤ **Make a plan.** Ask the teacher what can be done by both the teacher and the child to help solve the problem. It may be helpful to have the teacher call the parent if the problem happens again, in order to discuss possible solutions. Parents and teachers can look together at alternative short-term solutions. Often very young children may not understand what is expected of them in specific situations and may need added explanations and encouragement to meet a teacher's expectations. When young children understand the procedures to follow to complete a task, they may be better able to act without guidance. Knowing what to expect and what is expected of them increases children's ability to monitor their own behavior.

➤ **Plan follow-up communications.** Children are more likely to be concerned about improving their behavior if they believe their parents care about how they behave. When a parent shows enough concern to try a plan of action and then meet again with the teacher to evaluate its effectiveness, the parent sends a strong message to the child that he or she is expected to behave at school. It is sometimes beneficial to include the child in the follow-up conference, too, so that the child can make suggestions. Knowing that parents and teachers care enough to meet repeatedly about a problem may be more motivating than any material reward a child is offered.

WHEN THERE ARE NO APPARENT PROBLEMS

I N some cases, parent-teacher conferences may not be very informative, especially if the teacher reports that the child has no problems. Some parents may repeatedly hear that they "have nothing to worry about." While this may sound reassuring, these parents may come away without the necessary information to help their children continue to make steady progress in school. Children who are doing well scholastically and socially should still be the subject of a conference. The parents of these children may want to explore educational options for their children. Because the parent and the teacher may see two very different sides of the child, when the two get together to confer, they may realize an issue where there was not one readily apparent prior to the meeting. When parents anticipate that there will be no real issues discussed at a conference, they may want to be prepared to ask some of the following questions:

➤ **What does my child do that surprises you?** Very often this question can reveal to parents what expectations the teacher has for the child. Sometimes a child will behave quite differently at school than at home, so the parent may be surprised, as well.

➤ **What is my child reluctant to do?** This question may reveal to the parents more about the child's interests and dislikes than they would ordinarily know. The question may encourage the teacher to talk to the parent about the child's academic and social preferences.

➤ **What is a goal you would like to see my child achieve?** This question can serve as a springboard for parents and teachers to develop a plan to work together to help a child set and reach a specific outcome. Even well-behaved and high-achieving children may benefit from setting goals in areas that need improvement or in which they might excel.

➤ **What can I do at home to support what is being done at school?** This question is always appreciated. Teachers may have suggestions for parents but may be afraid to offer unsolicited advice. The question helps create a team feeling.

A Friendly Exchange

Meet with your child's teacher at the beginning of the year to discuss your respective expectations and hopes for the coming year. It would also be extremely helpful to exchange your contact information and the best times to be reached. You can give your child's teacher a card that she can keep on file. It may look something like this:

> My name is Jane Doe, and my husband's name is John. Please feel free to call us by our first names.
>
> My son's name is James, but he prefers to be called Jimmy.
>
> You can reach us at home before 9 A.M. or after 7 P.M. by phone at 212-555-5555. I often check my e-mail from work and at home in the evenings, so if it is convenient for you, you can write to me at my address, janedoe@myemail.com.

RESOLVING PARENT-TEACHER CONFLICTS

THERE will be inevitable occasions when parents and teachers will disagree. Some common topics of disagreement include curriculum, assignments, peer relationships, homework, and assessment. Just because a parent and teacher disagree does not mean that the child's educational success is destined to fail. It means that the team is having a setback, but with the correct strategies, communication, and procedures, the team can be put back on track. Some of these strategies include:

➤ **Know the school policy for addressing parent-teacher disagreements.** Teachers should check school and district policies for handling conflicts or disagreements with parents and should follow the procedures outlined.

➤ **Use discretion about when and where children and their families are discussed.** Resist temptations to discuss individual children and their families in inappropriate public or social situations.

➤ **Talk directly with the teacher about problems.** Address complaints directly to the teacher, either in person or by telephone, and then to other school personnel in the order specified by school policy. It is important to check the facts directly with the teacher before drawing conclusions.

➤ **Avoid criticizing the teacher in front of children.** Besides causing confusion and conflict, criticizing the teacher in front of the child does nothing to address the problem. Criticism may put a young child in a bind over divided loyalties. As children age, such criticism may foster arrogance, defiance, and rudeness toward teachers.

➤ **Choose an appropriate time and place to discuss disagreements.** Parents should keep in mind that the end of the day, when both teachers and parents are tired, is probably not the best time for a discussion involving strong feelings. If an extended discussion is needed, make an appointment with the teacher.

Using respect, tact, and grace, most parent-teacher conflicts can be resolved successfully. Many times these disagreements can be solved without a child being aware that there was a conflict at all. If a parent-teacher conflict requires escalation to the principal/administrator level, be sure to be organized, calm, and prepared. Also be sure to have open ears and an even more open mind.

MAKING IT ALL WORK TOGETHER

PARENTS and teachers work toward the same goals. Each strives to ensure the success of the student. Although you may occasionally feel as though you are on different sides of the fence, it is important to keep a gate of communicate open between you. The student, your child, is an important member of this educational team, although his role is not discussed in depth in this chapter. His social and academic growth throughout this year will be the gauge by which you judge the success of the team as a whole. Using the strategies outlined throughout this book should minimize misunderstandings and conflicts between the most important role models in your young child's life.

6

The 3rd Grade
Problem Solver

HOMEWORK, ugh! There is no faster way to get a discussion started among parents of third-grade children than to mention the dreaded "H" word! Grown adults have been seen holding their heads in their hands, frustrated with a child who hates homework, their own misunderstandings of the teacher's expectations, or puzzled with the "new" methods of working math problems. Homework is one of the few topics that often causes the same amount of frustration and dismay in parents as it does in children.

In the past your child's homework may have included practicing spelling words, completing worksheets, or gathering information (such as, "What is your address?"). This year your child will spend more time working independently. Your third grader may spend time reading a chapter in his social studies book, and then answering a series of context related questions at the end of the reading assignment. "Theme" projects are not unusual for the third grader. When learning about the solar system in Science, your child may also read a story about an astronaut in Reading and practice space-related words in Spelling (such as planet and astronaut).

Although most children will tell you that homework is not the most pleasant way they would like to spend their time, there are a lot of benefits to homework. Usually if an assignment is something more than busywork— something to which the child can really relate—and if parents are supportive and encourage the completion of the tasks, their child will benefit by gaining higher grades, better study habits, and a more positive attitude toward school and learning. Also, parents also should view homework as a window into their child's class work, subject matter, and curriculum.

WHY IS HOMEWORK IMPORTANT?

ADMITTEDLY most of us do not have fond memories of struggling with homework throughout our school career. For that reason, we often project those same negative feelings on our children. In the midst of our frustration, it is difficult for us to remember why it is important that our children have homework assignments. After all, they have already spent as many as six hours at school, working at the task of learning. Why should our third graders have to come home and continue that process?

Ongoing research has begun to focus on the relationship between academic achievement and homework. Although the findings over the past decade are mixed about whether homework actually increases academic achievement, many teachers and parents agree that homework develops students' initiative and responsibility and fulfills the expectations of students, parents, and the public. In general, homework assignments have been found to be most helpful if they are carefully planned by the teachers and have a direct meaning to the students.

Furthermore, more children today have personal difficulties that are associated with a host of problems in school, including the ability to complete homework successfully. These include:

➤ troubled or unstable home lives
➤ lack of positive adult role models
➤ a high rate of mobility, among families who move their children from school to school

According to some researchers, two ways to increase students' opportunities to learn are to increase the amount of time that students have to learn and to expand the amount of content they receive. Homework assignments may foster both these goals. Reforms in education have called for increased homework, and as a result, reports show that students are completing considerably more homework than they did a decade ago. According to statements by the National PTA and the National Education Association (NEA), children in kindergarten through third grade should receive no more than 20 minutes worth of homework per day. However, don't be concerned if this amount varies. Some students are slower or faster workers, and the amount of homework can depend on the type of assignment given.

Teachers assign homework for many reasons. Homework can help children:

➤ practice what they have learned in school
➤ get ready for the next day's class
➤ use resources, such as libraries and encyclopedias
➤ learn things they don't have time to learn in school

Homework can also help children learn good habits and attitudes. Some other reasons for assigning homework in the elementary grades are to teach children the fundamentals of working independently and to encourage self-discipline and responsibility, as assignments provide some youngsters with their first chance to manage time and meet deadlines.

COMMON HOMEWORK PROBLEMS AND SOLUTIONS

My third-grade son completes his homework when he gets home from school. I think that he rushes through it. He does a rather sloppy job of things, and I often have to make him redo his work. How can I get him to slow down?

Perhaps it is time to evaluate your son's homework personality. When he gets home from school, is he really prepared to do homework, or would he do better with a small break between coming home and starting his homework? Perhaps he is rushing because he would rather be outdoors playing, or watching his favorite program. You may want to try to give him a small break, perhaps let him have a snack and some play time. He could then work on his homework after supper, while you are cleaning up the kitchen.

Parents should understand that all children have their own unique homework personality. For example, a dad from Pennsylvania has two sons who have vastly differing homework personalities. The eldest son prefers to delve into his homework right after walking in the door and grabbing a snack. His younger son needs to debrief after school. He often plays until suppertime. After supper, he sets to work on his homework. While the older child is able to do his homework privately, without supervision, his younger brother needs a homework center in the middle of the house, where he is easily supervised, and finds help easily accessible. Some other things to keep in mind are:

➤ **Figure out how your child learns best.** Knowing this makes it easier for you to help your child. For example, if your child learns things best when he can see them, draw a picture or a chart to help with some assignments. But if your child learns best when he can handle things, an apple cut four ways can help him learn fractions. If you've never thought about this learning style, observe your child. Check with the teacher if you aren't sure.

➤ **Encourage good study habits.** See that your child schedules enough time for assignments and makes his own practice tests at home before a test. When a big research report is coming up, encourage him to use the library.

➤ **Talk about assignments and ask questions.** This helps your child think through an assignment and break it into small, workable parts. For example, ask if she understands the assignment, whether she needs help with the work, and if her answer makes sense to her.

➤ **Give praise.** People of all ages like to be told when they have done a good job. And give helpful criticism when your child hasn't done his best work so that he can improve.

Once I let him decide when to do his homework, the daily problems eased up.

—A MOM FROM CALIFORNIA

My daughter has a lot of homework. It often takes us at least an hour every night to complete her homework assignments! I think that this is too much for her, after all, she is just a third grader. Is this too much homework?

You will want to evaluate some things about your daughter's nightly homework load. Is her homework excessive, or is most of her time spent daydreaming or glancing up at the television? Similar to how we grownups track our budget by writing down each and every expense, right down to a pack of gum, you will want to keep track of the time your daughter spends on homework, in order to be sure that indeed the entire hour is spent on homework, and not other superfluous activities.

If, after you have monitored your daughter's homework time, you still believe that the problem is that she has too much homework, you should consider sharing any concerns you may have regarding the amount or type of homework assigned with your child's teacher or principal.

If your child is having trouble with homework:

➤ **Call or meet with the teacher.** For example, get in touch with the teacher if your child refuses to do assignments, or if you or your child can't understand the instructions, or if you can't help your child get organized to do the assignments.

➤ **Believe that the school and the teacher want to help you and your child.** Work together to fix or lessen the homework problem. Different problems require different solutions. For example:

- Does your child have a hard time finishing assignments on time? Perhaps he has poor study skills and needs help getting organized.
- Is the homework too hard? Maybe your child has fallen behind and needs special help from a teacher or a tutor.
- Is she bored with the homework? Perhaps it's too easy and your child needs extra assignments that give more challenge. Or perhaps she would be more interested if another way could be found for her to learn the same material. Remember that not all homework can be expected to interest your child. Most teachers, however, want to give homework that children enjoy

and can finish successfully, and they welcome comments from parents.

➤ Follow up. Touch base with the teacher and check in with your child to make sure the plan is working.

It seems that we spend a lot of time on the phone with my daughter's class-mates! So often, my daughter will have her basic assignment written down, but in some sort of third grader shorthand. Unfortunately, she forgets her own shorthand when she gets home, so we end up on the phone with her classmates, trying to decipher what the homework assignment really is. Help!

Encourage your child to take notes concerning homework assignments in case questions arise later at home. Many schools now offer assignment tablets for children to write down their homework assignments. If your school does not offer these assignment books, you might want to consider purchasing one yourself. Try to remind your daughter that she will need to not only write down the assignment (ex. Math, page 35), but also a little note about the assignment. Perhaps something like, (ex. Math, page 35. Work all odd problems, showing all work. Neatness counts.). Notes like this not only give her the actual assignment, but also give her enough information about the assignment so that she will know exactly what is expected of her. Remember that she may need help learning to take accurate notes about her homework assignments. Perhaps you could help her by giving her examples, and be sure to praise her when she brings home complete notes about her assignments.

Getting Ready

If you want to create a routine around homework time, get orga-nized. Take an old shoebox. Decorate it, cover it with paper and designs. Then, fill the box with all the supplies needed to complete homework, such as pencils, pens, paper, a ruler, markers, a dictio-nary, and a pencil sharpener. Keep the box in a designated spot until homework time. This way, your child will know that when the box is brought out, homework time begins and he will have everything he will need.

Now that my son is going to be starting third grade, I have heard from other parents that his homework will be more difficult. What sort of supplies should we have at home to help him with his homework?

Yes, it is true that third grade homework is a bit more difficult than homework of the previous school years. Your child is expected to work more independently than ever before, and to do that, he will need some tools. Try to provide a suitable study area and the necessary tools to complete the homework assignments. In order to best help your child with homework, make sure your child has:

> ➤ A quiet place to work with good light.
> ➤ A regular time each day for doing homework.
> ➤ Basic supplies, including paper, pencils, pens, markers, glue, and a ruler.

You may have to take a shopping trip to the local craft or department store if your child is working on a special project, such as a model of the solar system, to buy special, one-time-only supplies.

How can I help my third grader with his homework when I don't understand it?

Remember when your parents cried out the evils of "New Math?" They were often at a loss; they knew what the answer to the problem was, but not the methodology that the teachers wanted us to use to find the correct answer. Not understanding the homework, or the expectations of the teacher, often frustrate not only the student, but the parent as well.

How many parents have wrung their hands in dismay, chewed on pencils, and scribbled on scrap paper trying to figure out exactly what the child is supposed to do to complete the homework assignment? So, what do you do when you do not understand a homework assignment? Ask for help! Search out help from other parents, your child's classmates, or even friends who have children who may have recently worked on a similar assignment or project. If your child's teacher has given you a phone number or e-mail address that can be used to contact her, feel free to call and ask for clarification of the assignment. If the assignment is a long-term project, simply write a note to the teacher asking for help. Not only does this help you help your child, but it also shows your third grader that there are resources available, even when both of you are confused. Remember that the teacher is your teammate in your child's education. Your child's success is dependent on the willingness of the entire team to put forth a stellar effort. Because you are teammates, and have already entered into a cooperative relationship, the entire team wins with this sort of collaboration.

My son is involved in several after school activities. He takes part in cub scouts, several sports, and our local church youth group. These activities often start right after we get home from work and school. By the time we get home from his activities, then grab a quick bite to eat, it is time for a bath and bed-time. We often complete homework quickly at the end of the night, or in between activities. Is there a good way to balance activities and homework? I don't want him to give up any of his current extracurricular activities.

Balancing after-school activities and homework has become more of an issue for parents over the past decade. Today, children are more active in social, athletic, and religious activities than ever before. While these activities are very important and beneficial to a child's growth, it is important that parents do not allow their child to become overloaded. Third-grade children, while extremely energetic, need downtime built into their schedule. Also, they will thrive on routine. For these reasons, you should consider limiting after-school activities to allow time for both homework and family activities. Perhaps allow your child to be involved in one sport or activity at a time. Try not to schedule your child so that he has something going on every night of the week. Ideally, he should have at least one evening of leisure between each evening of activity. Remember, you are trying to build a well-rounded successful person, and he needs to know that his schoolwork is very important, not just something that can be worked in around all the other activities in his life.

My children go to after-school daycare. I pick them up on my way home from work. When we get home, I immediately start to cook dinner, while the children usually camp in front of the TV or video game console. We then have our dinner, and I have to fight with them to get to work on their home-work. Frankly, it is a battle that I am often too exhausted to fight by the time the dishes are being cleaned up. We often get to the homework in between baths and bedtime. What advice could help me?

Wow, this sounds like a very busy family. Perhaps it is possible for the children to complete their homework assignments, in part or in full, at the after-school daycare program they attend. If that is possible, you can encourage your children to work on their homework at after-school daycare, and then share the homework with you after dinner. This would allow them time to watch some television, play video games, or play together, while also affording you some time to prepare your evening meal. Going over homework after dinner can become a nightly event, time for all of you to spend together before baths and bedtime. Because third-grade children are still creatures of habit, it is important that parents monitor television viewing and establish a specific homework time. If your children are not able to do homework at their after-school daycare provider, consider having them work on it while you prepare your meal. Then, allow television and play time after dinner, when the entire family is able to relax and interact.

I find that my son often struggles with his homework. I look at him, sitting at the table, staring intently at his worksheets, trying so hard to figure out the answers. He works hard, is an average student, and never gives me much trouble. The problem is that he struggles so with his homework. I worry that he gets too

---

Consider your children's homework personalities, offer solutions to them, then plan a homework schedule with your children. Be sure that your children know that you will allow for free time when assignments are completed. To find out what works best for your child, observe your child for a week using the following worksheet.

Mood after school _____

Homework: self-starter or needed constant reminders?

Think of specific recent incidents to give a one-word description of your child's responses to homework _____

When challenged, my child _____

When frustrated, my child _____

When successful, my child _____

Time spent on

  Homework _____

  Reading (to self or being read to) _____

  Quiet play _____

  Active play _____

  Watching TV _____

  Computer use or video games _____

Ate for dinner _____

Mood in evening/at bedtime _____

frustrated. Also, I am not sure how much to help him. I don't want to do his homework for him.

The first thing that you should do is to give your child a hug and praise his efforts. The fact that he is working so hard on his homework is a testimony to you—and the learning environment in your home. If questions arise about the assignments, and your child asks for help, ask him questions or work through an example rather than simply providing the answer. Perhaps he only needs help seeing how to think about a problem. Never give the answers to a problem without having your child understand how the two of you came to the conclusion. Continue to encourage your child. As long as he sees that you care about his educational success, he will continue to thrive.

I know that many parents spend a lot of time helping their children with homework at night. I try to let my children do their homework on their own. How much help should I provide to my third grader when doing homework?

As you might imagine, younger children need more parental assistance with homework than older children. As your children get older, your interaction will wane. For now, you should go over homework assignments with your child. This will ensure that your child is clear about what is expected of him, and that you are kept informed about what he is covering in school. If your child is still unclear about the assignment, do several problems or questions together, then observe your child doing the next one or two. If all seems well, you should encourage him to complete the assignment on his own, allowing him to think through even the more difficult problems. Be sure that he knows that you are available to help him if he has any trouble with any of the questions. You should help him think through a problem, rather than just give him the answers.

Because I think that some of my daughter's grade is comprised of her homework, I am a bit confused. Specifically, should I correct my third grader's homework?

You should check with your child's teacher to see what she expects from you. The common rule of thumb is "Don't do the assignment yourself. It's not your homework—it's your child's." Of course, if your child has questions about her homework, feel free to help explain, and help her think through the problem, coming to her own conclusions. If her conclusion is obviously incorrect, help her think through it again, offering some of your own insights. No matter what grade your child is in, ask to look at homework once it has been marked and returned. As always, feel free to ask your child's teachers about their homework policy and specific assignments. How closely you watch over homework will depend on the age of your child, how independent she is, and how well she does in school. Some ways that you can give your third grader some gentle guidance are:

> **Ask what the teacher expects.** At the start of the school year, find out what kinds of assignments will be given and how the teacher wants you involved. Some teachers only want you to make sure the assignment is completed. Others want parents to go over the homework and point out mistakes.

> **Check to see that assignments are started and finished on time.** If you aren't home when the homework is finished, look it over when you get home.

> **Monitor TV viewing and other activities.** In most homes, more homework gets done when TV time is limited. See that things like music lessons or basketball don't take too much time. If homework isn't getting done, your child may need to drop an activity.

What can I do to help my third grader have a good homework experience?

Show your child that you think education and homework are important. Children are more eager to do homework if they know their parents care that it gets done. Some helpful tips to ensure that you are setting the right homework tone in your house are:

> **Set a regular time for homework.** The best time is one that works for your child and your family.

> **Pick a place to study that is fairly quiet and has lots of light.** A desk is nice. But the kitchen table or a corner of the living room can work just fine.

> **Help your child concentrate.** Turn off the TV and say no to telephone calls during homework time. If you live in a small or noisy

household, have all family members take part in a quiet activity during homework time. You may need to take a noisy toddler outside to play or into another room.

➤ **Gather materials.** Collect papers, books, pencils, and other things your child needs to do homework. Tell the teacher or school counselor or principal if you need help getting your child these things.

➤ **Set a good example by reading and writing yourself.** Your child learns what things are important by watching what you do. Encourage educational activities. Go on walks in the neighborhood, trips to the zoo, and encourage chores that teach responsibility.

➤ **Read with your child.** This activity stimulates interest in reading and language and lays the foundation for your child to become a lifelong reader.

➤ **Take your child to the library.** Encourage him to check out materials needed for homework. Talk about school and learning activities. Attend school activities, such as parent-teacher meetings and sports events.

Model Behavior

If your child is uninspired by sitting down to do homework, model good behavior to show him you care. Take his homework time as an opportunity to sit and pay your bills, complete work from the office, or to write those letters you've been meaning to send to old friends. You might find that you will both get a lot of work done.

Last year in third grade, my daughter kept "forgetting" she had homework, or she'd tell us it was done. If I would ask to see it she would say she did it at school and left it there. I wanted to believe her, so I would give her the benefit of the doubt and then find out she had not turned her homework in. It was never that she could not do it, just that she did not want to.

We were in contact with the teacher and we discussed her problem. When my daughter realized that both her parents and her teacher were involved, she understood that homework was important and she would not get away with not doing it. Seeing our concern, she improved by the end of the year.

—A PARENT FROM NEW JERSEY

My daughter has a case of the "I forgot syndrome." It seems that she never remembers to bring home her homework. If she remembers to bring it home, she forgets to return it. If she remembers both of those, she forgets what the assignment was. It seems that she generally has trouble staying organized.

Sometimes we have to step back and realize that although our third graders would like us to believe that they are grown up, they are really only eight or nine years old. Some of us who are much older still have trouble maintaining organization. For those reasons, it is the job of the grownups in our children's lives to show them how to become organized. Some questions that you may want to ask your third grader include:

➤ What's your assignment today?
➤ Is the assignment clear? (If not, suggest calling the school's homework hotline or a classmate.)
➤ When is it due?
➤ Do you need special resources (e.g., a trip to the library or access to a computer)?
➤ Do you need special supplies (e.g., graph paper or poster board)?
➤ Have you started today's assignment? Finished it?
➤ Is it a long-term assignment (e.g., a report or science project)?
➤ For a major project, would it help to write out the steps or make a schedule?
➤ Would a practice test be useful?

CHECKLIST FOR HELPING YOUR CHILD WITH HOMEWORK

THE United States Department of Education has surmised that there are four major keys to homework success. These keys include a mixture of common sense, participation, and attention on the part of the parent. There are some basic rules that we can all follow to foster a healthy attitude toward homework. The following checklist should help you and your third grader make the most of one of the least favorite school activities—homework!

MONITOR ASSIGNMENTS

DO not assume that your child is doing well with his homework. Studies have shown that children are more likely to complete assignments if their parents monitor homework. The third grader becomes easily distracted, and may require a gentle reminder to keep him on track. Be aware of feedback from his teacher. Her comments on corrected homework assignments will help guide you and your third grader toward the path to success. Under your watch, he will receive help with subjects he is struggling with, and praise for a job well done! Consider the following:

- ❑ Do you know what your child's homework assignments are?
- ❑ How long they should take?
- ❑ How does the teacher want you to be involved?
- ❑ Do you see that assignments are started and completed?
- ❑ Do you read the teacher's comments on assignments that are returned?
- ❑ Is TV viewing cutting into your child's homework time?

PROVIDE GUIDANCE

REMEMBER that your third grader will look to you for direction with homework completion. At school she has a teacher who explains the rules for everything from bathroom breaks, to where your child's name should appear on her class work. Parental guidance with homework has become more necessary as many teachers are assigning the tasks for the entire week at the beginning of the week, allowing the parent and child to work at their own pace.

- ❑ Do you understand and respect your child's style of learning? Does he work better alone or with someone else? Does he learn best when he can see things, hear them, or handle them?

❑ Do you help your child to get organized? Does your child need a calendar or assignment book? A bag for books and a folder for papers?

❑ Do you encourage your child to develop good study habits (e.g., scheduling enough time for big assignments; making up practice tests)?

❑ Do you talk with your child about homework assignments? Does she understand them?

TALK WITH SOMEONE AT SCHOOL WHEN PROBLEMS COME UP

YOUR involvement with your third grader's education will help you meet any homework problems head-on. Chances are, because you have established a relationship with the teacher, you will feel comfortable discussing any difficulties that you or your child may have with the content, frequency, or quantity of homework. Having an open relationship with the school teachers and administrators also will give you a clear view of the school's homework policies. Consider the following:

❑ Do you meet the teacher early in the year *before* any problems arise?

❑ If a problem comes up, do you meet with the teacher?

❑ Do you cooperate with the teacher and your child to work out a plan and a schedule to fix homework problems?

❑ Do you follow up with the teacher and with your child to make sure the plan is working?

At a workshop I went to last week, one idea that worked well . . . was to assign the week's homework on Monday with different assignments due different days of the week. So the kids knew when each assignment was due, some went ahead and did it all and got it out of the way, while others doled it out. Interesting, I thought.

—A TEACHER AND PARENT FROM MICHIGAN

No matter how involved we parents are, no matter how many of the guidelines listed above are followed, no matter how wonderful our attitudes, homework is never going to be ranked as a child's favorite thing about school. We should not even try to fool ourselves into believing that we will raise homework-loving children. What we should strive to do is to raise children who view homework as a necessary part of learning, who understand the benefits, and ultimately begin to view homework as a tool used to support the daily lessons learned in the classroom.

Be sure to supply your child with all the supplies necessary to do their job. Imagine if you were expected to show up at your job, only to find that you were missing half of the tools necessary to your profession. It would cause you to become very frustrated, and perhaps encourage a negative attitude toward work. Remember that your child's homework is his job; not having the correct supplies to do the job at hand will undoubtedly provoke the same negative reactions in your child.

It is also very advantageous to make time to take your child to the library to check out materials needed for homework, and read with your child as often as you can. Talk about school and learning activities in family conversations. Ask your child what was discussed in class that day. If he doesn't have much to say, try another approach. For example, ask your child to read aloud a story he wrote or discuss the results of a science experiment.

Most importantly, face homework with a positive attitude, understand your child's homework personality, and make homework into a serene time that you and your child can share within the chaos of your hustle and bustle day.

7

On Gifted and Learning Disabled Children

THROUGHOUT this book, we have talked about the average third grader, while touching on just a few of the traits that may make your child unique. As all parents know, there are very few children who actually fit the complete description of the "average" child. Each child has their own set of strengths and weaknesses, which are also influenced by that child's environment, opportunities, and their individual passions and interests. For this reason, it is important that we talk a bit more about the not-so-average child.

Some children have needs that are not fulfilled within the bounds of the standard third-grade curriculum. These children are most often identified as belonging to one of two groups—the gifted child or the learning disabled child. The children in the gifted group are often high achievers, or talented children who will require extra stimulation. The children who become identified as learning disabled may be a bit behind, have unique learning styles, or special emotional, psychological, or academic needs that cause them to have difficulty learning in a conventional classroom environment. There is also a third group, the gifted but learning disabled child. One of the emotions common to children in each of these groups is frustration.

Third grade is often a threshold year. As the teaching and learning styles evolve from play learning to work learning, and reading becomes stressed across the curriculum, giftedness and learning disabilities become more apparent. The parent who is actively involved with their child and his or her education will also notice if their child needs help outside of the general school curriculum, whether for gifted enrichment classes, or for remedial education. Having already built an open relationship with your child's educational team, you may already have the necessary information to correctly assess your child's needs and talents. Open, frank discussion with the other members of your child's educational team will help you lay out the proper course, no matter what your child's needs may be.

THE GIFTED CHILD

IN 1969, Congress mandated a study by the U.S. Commissioner of Education to determine the extent to which the needs of gifted and talented children were being met. The document published in response to this study was "The Marland Report," published in 1972. "The Marland Report" contains a definition of giftedness that has been and continues to be the one most widely adopted or adapted by state and local education agencies. The Report states: "Gifted and talented children are those identified by professionally qualified persons who, by virtue of outstanding abilities, are capable of high performance. These are children who require differential educational programs and/or services beyond those provided by the regular school program in order to realize their contribution to self and the society."

The U.S. Department of Education defines giftedness as "children or youth who give evidence of high performance capability in areas such as intellectual, creative, artistic, or leadership capacity, or in specific academic fields, and who require services or activities not ordinarily provided by the school in order to fully develop such capabilities."

Using these broad definitions of giftedness, a school system could expect to identify 10 percent to 15 percent or more of its student population as gifted and talented, depending on which study one refers to. Many parents wrestle

SOME OF THE EARLIEST SIGNS OF GIFTEDNESS INCLUDE:

- Abstract reasoning and problem-solving skills
- Curiosity
- Early and extensive language development
- Early recognition of caretakers (for example, smiling)
- Enjoyment and speed of learning
- Excellent sense of humor
- Extraordinary memory
- High activity level
- Intense reactions to noise, pain, or frustration
- Less need for sleep in infancy
- Long attention span
- Sensitivity and compassion
- Unusual alertness in infancy
- Vivid imagination (for example, imaginary companions)
- Advanced progression through developmental milestones

with themselves, trying to decide if their child is an excellent student, or if their child is indeed gifted. When asking yourself if you believe your child is gifted, you should ask yourself if, during the early years, your child exhibited some of the earliest signs of giftedness.

SHOULD MY CHILD BE EVALUATED?

Although it may be difficult to recall the exact age that a child reached the developmental milestones that will sometimes give the first clues of giftedness, most parents of a gifted child will be able to remember certain events that occurred when the child was young; events that stood out as being out of the norm for a child of that age. Typically, a parent will begin to see more concrete signs of giftedness as a child prepares for, and later attends, elementary school. The parent may notice that their child is able to quickly and correctly complete assignments, may discuss the day's learning in great detail, or can always be found reading books—often times at a higher grade level than expected.

Although it is obvious that no child is outstanding in all characteristics there are some other typical factors stressed by educational authorities as being indicative of giftedness. A gifted child often:

➤ Shows superior reasoning powers and marked ability to handle ideas; can generalize readily from specific facts and can see subtle relationships; has outstanding problem-solving ability.

➤ Shows persistent intellectual curiosity; asks searching questions; shows exceptional interest in the nature of man and the universe.

➤ Has a wide range of interests, often of an intellectual kind; develops one or more interests to considerable depth.

➤ Is markedly superior in quality and quantity of written and/or spoken vocabulary; is interested in the subtleties of words and their uses.

➤ Reads avidly and absorbs books well beyond his or her years.

➤ Learns quickly and easily and retains what is learned; recalls important details, concepts and principles; comprehends readily.

➤ Shows insight into arithmetical problems that require careful reasoning and grasps mathematical concepts readily.

➤ Shows creative ability or imaginative expression in such things as music, art, dance, drama; shows sensitivity and finesse in rhythm, movement, and bodily control.

➤ Sustains concentration for lengthy periods and shows outstanding responsibility and independence in classroom work.

➤ Sets realistically high standards for self; is self-critical in evaluating and correcting his or her own efforts.

➤ Shows initiative and originality in intellectual work; shows flexibility in thinking and considers problems from a number of viewpoints.

➤ Observes keenly and is responsive to new ideas.

➤ Shows social poise and an ability to communicate with adults in a mature way.

➤ Gets excitement and pleasure from intellectual challenge; shows an alert and subtle sense of humor.

If your child is exhibiting many of these characteristics, you may wish to schedule a meeting with the other members of your child's educational team to discuss the gifted assessment process.

When studying giftedness in children, the United States Department of Education has found that firstborn children tend to be recognized as gifted or talented more often than their siblings. It is also important to note that when one child in the family is gifted, it is quite possible that others may also be gifted. Most educators recommend early identification (ages three through eight) because it permits early intervention, which is just as important for gifted children as for any other children with special needs.

INTERACTION WITH THE GIFTED CHILD

GENERALLY, the gifted child will thrive in an environment where his special talents are challenged appropriately. The gifted child will need some direction from the adults around him. Parents, teachers, and special enrichment staff should be prepared to recognize the particular needs of the child, and work together to map out an appropriate plan for success.

Because so many gifted children are verbally and linguistically advanced, parents of gifted children sometimes need to be reminded that it is important that they continue to read aloud to their gifted child, even books that the child is already capable of reading. Reading aloud to the gifted child not only expands the child's literary and verbal horizons, it also allows the child to think about circumstances, solve puzzles, or consider things from a different point of view. This type of higher, deeper thinking is important to keep the gifted child from being bored.

Third-grade gifted children may require the assistance of their parents and teachers with discovering personal interests. Stimulation and support of interests are vital to the development of talents. The proactive parent may expose their child to their own interests, while encouraging the child to explore a wide variety of subjects, such as art, nature, music, and sports. In addition to sharing and encouraging the arts and athletics, some traditional academic subjects, such as math, reading, and science, may also hold a third grader's interest. For that reason, it is important that the parent of a third-grade gifted child be open and aware to their child's needs and passions.

If you are the parent of a gifted child, encourage the support of extended family and friends. As an infant, your gifted child may have exhausted you because he or she often slept less than other babies and required extra stimulation when awake. As a school-aged child, the gifted child may entertain himself for long stretches of time, but may also need new challenges, new questions, new answers, and new interests at an almost feverish pace. As parents of the latter, you may find it helpful to have extended family, such as grandparents who live nearby, or close friends in the neighborhood who can spend some time with the child so that the precocious third grader receives added—or different—stimulation. The change of scenery and knowledge also allow the gifted third grader to become exposed to a plethora of information, stimulation, and conversation—all of which are very important to the growth of the successful gifted child.

Although all children deserve to be spoken to and listened to with consideration and respect, it is especially important for the gifted child. From the time he or she can talk, a gifted child is constantly asking questions and will often challenge authority. "Do it because I said so" doesn't work. The child wants to know the logical reasons behind any requests or demands, and is usually not shy about asking for a complete and thorough explanation. For this reason it important that the parents of gifted children understand that generally, a gifted child will cooperate more with parents who take the time to explain requests than with more authoritarian parents.

CHALLENGING THE GIFTED CHILD

THERE are many ways that parents can ensure that their gifted child is kept busy, happy, and enriched. Some of these children will thrive taking music lessons, participating in sports, or perhaps by taking language classes. After a child is identified as gifted, the child's school will often schedule a meeting to discuss the needs of the child, as well as the child's strengths and weaknesses. At this meeting, parents, teachers, and possibly other members of a child's educational team will also discuss possible courses of action necessary for a child to maintain a healthy interest in learning, as well as to provide the child with a fertile learning environment.

Some enrichment goals that you may provide to your gifted child are:

- Exposure to new and challenging information about the environment and culture
- Exposure to varied subjects and concerns
- Permission and encouragement to pursue ideas as far as their interests take them
- Exposure and conversation using increasingly difficult vocabulary and concepts
- Exposure to ideas at rates appropriate to the individual's pace of learning
- The time to pursue inquiries beyond allotted time spans
- Access to intellectual peers

- In depth verbal exchange of ideas
- A longer incubation time for ideas
- Encouragement to creatively and imaginatively pursue new ideas, without expecting the child to produce a solution or finished product
- To build skills in productive thinking
- To draw generalizations and test them

Again, according to veteran third-grade teacher, Carolyn Kneas, the third-grade gifted child is usually a voracious reader. The third-grade gifted child may have begun to recognize books by author, and will likely choose library books according to either author, or topic. Because of this high interest in reading, parents will find that books are usually a welcome tool to challenging the gifted third grader. Refer back to Chapter 3 in this book for ideas on supplementing your child's education. Also, there are some great resources, including books, software, and websites in the Resources Section.

However, there are some ways that well-meaning parents kill creativity in gifted children. These include:

➤ **Insisting that children do things the "right way."** Teaching a child to think that there is just one right way to do things kills the urge to try new ways.

➤ **Pressuring children to be realistic, to stop imagining.** When we label a child's flights of fantasy as "silly," we bring the child down to earth with a thud, causing the inventive urge to subside.

➤ **Making comparisons with other children.** This is a subtle pressure on a child to conform; yet the essence of creativity is freedom to conform or not to conform.

➤ **Discouraging children's curiosity.** One of the surest indicators of creativity is curiosity; yet we often brush questions aside because we are too busy for "silly" questions. Children's questions deserve respect.

SCHOOL PLACEMENT

SO often parents struggle with leaving their child at the grade level representative of their child's chronological age, or advancing their gifted child to a grade representative of their intellectual age. At the third-grade level it has been found that a child in a classroom of mixed-aged groupings, benefits as long as the gifted child is not the oldest in the group. Gifted, creative boys are often held back in the primary years because of so-called immaturity.

Acceleration, also known as grade advancement, may be considered when a school offers insufficient challenges or when gifted children are not grouped with peers their age who are intellectually advanced. Before accelerating a child, the child's entire educational team should consider the following question: "Is this child both socially and intellectually prepared and capable of moving to a classroom of intellectual, and not necessarily chronological, peers?" Also keep in mind, when a child expresses a willingness to be accelerated, chances are good that he or she will make an appropriate social adjustment.

More important, a child's educational program should be designed to foster progress at the child's rate of development. The involved parent can help administrators and teachers be responsive to the needs of their higher need, gifted child.

A FINAL WORD ON THE GIFTED CHILD

PARENTS of gifted children need opportunities to share parenting experiences with one another. Be sure to seek out other parents of gifted children in your school, school district, and regional area. Keeping the provisions provided to gifted children in place takes the persistence and enthusiasm of large groups of parents. It is important for parents of children with any special needs, including giftedness, to meet with teachers early in the school year, work regularly with teachers, and stay both involved in their child's education and informed about gifted education in general.

The key to raising gifted children is to respect their uniqueness, their opinions and ideas, and their dreams. It can be painful for parents when their children feel out of sync with others, but it is unwise to put too much emphasis on the importance of fitting in; children get enough of that message in the outside world. At home, children need to know that they are appreciated for being themselves.

THE LEARNING DISABLED CHILD

ACCORDING to recent research conducted by the National Institutes of Health, 15 to 20 percent of the U.S. population has some form of learning disability. The term learning disabled encompasses a wide array of difficulties a child may encounter throughout their educational career. These learning disabilities range from the very mild, to the extremely severe. A definition of learning disabilities developed in 1990 by the National Joint Committee on Learning Disabilities (NJCLD) reads as follows:

The National Institutes of Mental Health (NIMH) describes learning disabilities as:

"Learning Disabilities (LD) is a disorder that affects people's ability to either interpret what they see and hear or to link information from different parts of the brain. These limitations can show up in many ways—as specific difficulties with spoken and written language, coordination, self-control, or attention. Such difficulties extend to schoolwork and can impede learning to read or write, or to do math. Learning disabilities can be lifelong conditions that, in some cases, affect many parts of a person's life: school or work, daily routines, family life, and sometimes even friendships and play. In some people, many overlapping learning disabilities may be apparent. Other people may have a single, isolated learning problem that has little impact on other areas of their lives."

The major types of LD may be broken into disorders in four areas:

➤ Spoken language: delays, disorders, and deviations in listening and speaking
➤ Written language: difficulties with reading, writing, and spelling
➤ Arithmetic: difficulty in performing arithmetic functions or in comprehending basic concepts
➤ Reasoning: difficulty in organizing and integrating thoughts

SHOULD MY CHILD BE EVALUATED?

THIS checklist, created by The National Center for Learning Disabilities, is intended as a guidepost for parents and professionals. It should not be used in isolation, but may lead the parent or professional to seek further assessment. All children exhibit one or more of these behaviors from time to time throughout their childhood. A consistent showing of a group of these behaviors should be considered an indication to seek further advice, observation, or assessment.

DOES YOUR CHILD HAVE DIFFICULTY WITH:

ORGANIZATION
- ❑ knowing time, date, year
- ❑ managing time
- ❑ completing assignments
- ❑ organizing thoughts
- ❑ locating belongings
- ❑ carrying out a plan
- ❑ making decisions
- ❑ setting priorities
- ❑ sequencing

PHYSICAL COORDINATION
- ❑ manipulating small objects
- ❑ learning self-help skills
- ❑ cutting
- ❑ drawing
- ❑ handwriting
- ❑ climbing and running
- ❑ mastering sports

SPOKEN OR WRITTEN LANGUAGE
- ❑ pronouncing words
- ❑ learning new vocabulary
- ❑ following directions
- ❑ understanding requests
- ❑ relating stories
- ❑ discriminating among sounds
- ❑ responding to questions
- ❑ understanding concepts
- ❑ reading comprehension
- ❑ spelling
- ❑ writing stories and essays

ATTENTION OR CONCENTRATION
- ❑ completing a task
- ❑ acting before thinking
- ❑ poor organization
- ❑ waiting
- ❑ restlessness
- ❑ daydreaming
- ❑ distractibility

MEMORY
- ❑ remembering directions
- ❑ learning math facts
- ❑ learning new procedures
- ❑ learning the alphabet
- ❑ identifying letters
- ❑ remembering names
- ❑ remembering events
- ❑ spelling
- ❑ studying for tests

SOCIAL BEHAVIOR
- ❑ making and keeping friends
- ❑ social judgment
- ❑ impulsive behavior
- ❑ frustration tolerance
- ❑ sportsmanship
- ❑ accepting changes in routine
- ❑ interpreting nonverbal cues
- ❑ working cooperatively

—From the National Center for Learning Disabilities, Inc.

Students who are learning disabled may exhibit a wide range of traits, including poor reading comprehension, spoken language, writing, and reasoning ability. Hyperactivity, inattention, and perceptual coordination problems may also be associated with learning disabilities, but are not examples of a learning disability. Other traits that may be present in a child with a learning disability include a variety of symptoms of brain dysfunction, including uneven and unpredictable test performance, perceptual impairments, motor disorders, and emotional characteristics such as impulsiveness, low tolerance for frustration, and maladjustment.

YOUR INITIAL REACTION

WHILE the parent who has just found out that their child has been evaluated and labeled "gifted" is usually quick to share the news, and strides through the day with a beaming smile, the parent of a learning-disabled child is often filled with many emotions, many fears, and many questions. The parent of a newly diagnosed learning-disabled child may be wracked with guilt, and filled with questions like "What could I have done differently?" Other parents in the same situation may exhale a huge sigh of relief, finally knowing that there really is a reason for their child's lower level of performance. The weight of the unknown is lifted, and finally they feel emancipated and ready to take action. No matter what your initial reaction may be upon being notified of your child's learning disability, it is most beneficial to you, your child, and your child's educational success, if you become knowledgeable and focused on your child's specific disability.

There is a lot to understand about learning disabilities. Learning disabilities, which often run in families, are lifelong conditions that can be manifested in different ways during the school years. Children with learning disabilities, however, can compensate for their difficulties with appropriate intervention, support, and accommodations. A good website to begin your research about your child's learning disability is www.ldonline.com.

Today's society has become very focused on attention deficits and hyperactivity disorders. While these conditions sometimes occur with learning disabilities, it is important to know that learning disabilities, Attention Deficit Disorder (ADD) and Attention Deficit Hyperactivity Disorder (ADHD) are not always concurrent conditions. It is also important that parents and children understand that learning disabilities have distinct characteristics and should not be confused with the following handicaps: mental retardation, autism, deafness, blindness, and behavioral disorders.

Identifying and diagnosing the child with a learning disability at an early age is vital to a child's educational success. The longer that a learning disability goes undiagnosed, and therefore without intervention, the higher the chances of the child suffering serious consequences. These consequences include loss of self-esteem, which can eventually lead to a poor attitude toward school. Left unidentified through the educational career, learning disabilities can contribute to school drop-out, illiteracy, and other critical problems.

YOU ARE YOUR CHILD'S ADVOCATE

NOW that you know that your child has a special need, it is your responsibility to be sure that every member of the educational team is aware of the learning disability, and that all team members are ready to address the learning disability head on. There are some general guidelines that you can follow to ensure that the entire team is focused on your child's success.

> ➤ **Develop a partnership.** Foster open communication with the school and share relevant information about your child's education and development. Ask for clarification of any aspect of the program that is unclear to you.
>
> ➤ **Make sure you understand the program specified in the Individual Education Plan (IEP).** The IEP is a written document that is developed at a meeting of the educational team. Federal law requires that the IEP be developed and reviewed annually. Take the IEP form home so that you can review it before you sign it. You have ten school days in which to make a decision and return the IEP documents.
>
> ➤ **Advocate for appropriate inclusion.** Consider and discuss with your child's teacher how your child might be included in the regular school activities program. Do not forget areas such as lunch, recess, art, music, and physical education.
>
> ➤ **Monitor your child's progress and ask for reports.** If your child is not progressing, discuss this with the teacher and determine whether the program should be modified.

➤ **Solve problems.** Discuss with the school any problems that occur with your child's assessment, placement, or educational program. If you are uncertain about how to resolve a problem, you can turn to the advocacy agencies found in most states for the guidance you need to pursue your case.

➤ **Keep records.** There may be many questions and comments about your child that you will want to discuss, as well as meetings and phone conversations you will want to remember.

➤ **Join a parent organization.** In addition to giving parents an opportunity to share knowledge and gain support, a parent group can be an effective force on behalf of your child.

THE GIFTED AND LEARNING DISABLED CHILD

NOW that we have discussed both the gifted child, and the child affected by any one of many learning disabilities, it is time to discuss the third type of child that falls outside of the "average" range. There is a percentage of our society that fits the definition of a gifted but learning disabled child. The gifted but learning disabled child presents a difficult challenge to all members of the educational team.

Who Are The Learning Disabled/Gifted?

Recent advances in both fields, learning disabled and gifted, have alerted professionals to the possibility that both sets of behavior can exist simultaneously. Children who are both gifted and learning disabled exhibit remarkable talents or strengths in some areas and disabling weaknesses in others. They can be grouped into three categories:

➤ identified gifted students who have subtle learning disabilities
➤ unidentified students whose gifts and disabilities may be masked by average achievement
➤ identified learning disabled students who are also gifted

IDENTIFIED GIFTED WHO HAVE SUBTLE
LEARNING DISABILITIES

THIS type of child is easily identified as gifted because of high achievement or high IQ scores. As this child grows older, his actual performance may not meet the expected performance of a child of such talent. This student may impress teachers with his verbal abilities, while his spelling or handwriting contradicts the image. This child may be sloppy, disorganized, or may seem disinterested. As these children get older, concerned adults are convinced that if these students would only try harder, they could succeed.

While increased effort may be required for these students, the real issue is that parents and educators simply do not know how. Because a child in this group may be on grade level and is considered gifted, she is likely to be overlooked for screening procedures necessary to identify a subtle learning disability. Identification of a subtle disability helps students understand why they are experiencing academic difficulties. More important, the entire educational team—parents, teachers, and enrichment staff—could offer learning strategies and compensation techniques to help them deal with the child's duality of learning behaviors.

A word of caution is necessary at this point. While learning disabilities can certainly impair the bright child, a learning disability is not and should not be considered to be the only cause of a discrepancy between potential and achievement. There are a number of other reasons why bright children may be underachieving. Perhaps the expectations for this child are unrealistic. Excelling in science, for example, is no assurance that high-level performance will be shown in other academic areas. Motivation, interest, and specific aptitudes influence the amount of energy students are willing to apply to a given task. Parents should also consider social or emotional problems that can take a toll on a child's level of achievement.

UNIDENTIFIED STUDENTS

THERE is a group of students who may have this combination of learning disabilities/giftedness who are never noticed. While their superior intellectual ability is working overtime to compensate for the learning disability, the learning disability masks the actual level of giftedness present in this child. In essence, their gift masks the disability and the disability masks the gift. These students are struggling to stay at grade level. These students are often difficult to find because they do not flag the need for attention by exceptional behavior. Their hidden talents and abilities may emerge in specific content areas or may be stimulated by a classroom teacher who uses a creative approach to learning. While children of all levels may have this mixture of gift and disability, it usually remains undiscovered until college or adulthood when the student happens to read about dyslexia or hears peers describe their learning difficulties.

IDENTIFIED LEARNING-DISABLED STUDENTS WHO ARE ALSO GIFTED

WITHIN most every school, there is a bright child who is identified as learning disabled. This child is often failing in school, and thus becomes labeled as learning disabled. This child first attracts attention because of a seeming lack of ability, rather than because of the talent they are demonstrating. This group of students is most at risk because of the stigma that accompanies the learning-disabled categorization that there is something wrong with the student that must be fixed before anything else can happen. Then entire educational team becomes focused on what the child cannot do, and negates any positive learning behaviors or talents displayed by the child. For this reason, most of the child's strengths or interests are not developed or encouraged, other than as a tool to compensate for the weakness.

Adding to the stigma, research has shown that this group of students is often rated by teachers as disruptive. These students are frequently found to be off task. This type of child may act out, daydream, or complain of headaches and stomachaches. This child is also easily frustrated and will use their creative abilities to avoid tasks. Since the conventional school learning environment does not offer these bright youngsters much opportunity to polish and use their gifts, such results are not surprising.

Because the school atmosphere may not present this child with the proper learning environment, parents should be extra sensitive to this child's needs and interests. Also, the parent of this child must be prepared to focus on the child's abilities, rather than his inabilities. With a little focus, a parent may realize that this child performs certain types of tasks at an amazingly high level. For instance, he may build fantastic structures with plastic bricks, create beautiful paintings, or start a local campaign to save the whales. The creative abilities, intellectual strength and passion they bring to their hobbies are clear indicators of their potential for giftedness. This child will, because of his giftedness, be acutely aware of his learning disability. It will be hard for him to maintain a positive attitude while feeling so inadequate. Over time, without the proper encouragement, this child may become pessimistic and sullen.

YOUR UNIQUE CHILD

SEVEN chapters ago, we started on a quest to discover more about the third-grade intellect, emotion, and experience. The first chapter started with a section discussing the uniqueness of your third grader. Along the way we have talked about the wonderful world of curriculum, the third-grade social butterfly, and even homework. The educational team was uncovered, and parental involvement in all aspects of a child's education was strongly encouraged; after all, we are the teachers of our tomorrow. Most importantly, we have basked in the vibrancy, energy, and curiosity found in most third-grade children.

Ah! There, I said it, "most" third-grade children. Among the collage of children found frolicking on the playground is your third grader, and most parents would agree that their third grader does not fit in the category of "most." Now we are winding down, and it seems that the message of each child's uniqueness seems to bear repeating. Only you know the mannerisms, nuances, and gifts that make your child special; a treasure. Hold that treasure dear to you, be involved in the education of that treasure, understand the strengths, the weaknesses, and the potential of that treasure. Celebrate your child. If your child is gifted, stretch his mind and his horizons. If your child has a learning disability, take stock in knowing that even Goliath had a weakness.

Some closing tips:

- Be your child's best advocate
- Pay attention to not only the spoken, but also the unspoken
- Enjoy your child's education, it is good for both of you

Resources:
The Best "Stuff" for 3rd Graders

CLEARLY, you want nothing but the best for your child and her education. For this reason, we have compiled a list of the best books, magazines, websites, CD-ROMs, and television programming available for your child. This list is not meant to be exhaustive, but it will be a great start for helping your child continue learning outside of the classroom.

You will also find a section of resources for parents of third graders. These books and websites contain information related to specific topics addressed in this book. In addition, these are great sites not only to find more information, but to express ideas about what has worked best for you as a parent.

BEST BOOKS FOR 3rd GRADERS

AS your child becomes an independent reader, you may find yourself needing to provide titles to your child. (And we hope this is the case.) For this reason, we have listed the following books that we are sure your child will enjoy and that you may even enjoy reading together.

Anne of Green Gables, by L. M. Montgomery (Bantam, Doubleday, Dell 1991)
Bridge to Terabithia, by Katherine Paterson (HarperTrophy, 1987)
Bud, Not Buddy, by Christopher Paul Curtis (Delacorte, 1999)
Charlotte's Web, by E. B. White (HarperCollins, 1987)
Harriet the Spy, by Louise Fitzhugh (HarperTrophy, 1990)
James and the Giant Peach, by Roald Dahl (Penguin, 1961)
Lincoln: A Photobiography, by Russell Freedman (Clarion, 1992)
Matilda, by Roald Dahl (Viking, 1988)
Missing May, by Cynthia Rylant (Yearling, 1993)

CHOOSING THE RIGHT BOOKS FOR YOUR CHILD'S READING LEVEL

Whenever possible, let your child choose his own reading materials at the library or bookstore (with your supervision, of course). If he is drawn to a book, so much the better! Allow plenty of time for browsing, and encourage your child to look at several pages of the book, rather than choosing one based on a title or cover image. Look for these three elements inside the book:

▪ **Pictures.** In general, the higher the reading level, the fewer the pictures. But keep in mind, many books for readers of this level do still contain some illustrations.

▪ **Chapters.** Chapter books are usually introduced to children gradually, starting sometime in the first grade. A short novel—that is, a book-length story told over the course of several chapters—is usually thought to be at appropriate level. The more chapters in a book, the higher the level.

▪ **Words per page.** The number of words on a page is a good indicator of its reading level. If a book is long on illustrations, and short on text, it is likely too easy for your third grader.

Take *all* these factors into account as you evaluate a particular book.

Most children won't voluntarily pick a book that is far beyond their level of comprehension—few of us seek out failure or frustration—unless the subject is one of passionate interest to them. In these cases, be willing to go along for the read. It's worth it.

—From *Reading Tutor*, by Mary Kay Linge (LearningExpress, 2000)

Number the Stars, by Lois Lowry (Yearling, 1990)

Ramona Quimby, Age 8, by Beverly Cleary (Morrow, 1981)

Sarah, Plain and Tall, by Patricia MacLachlan (HarperTrophy, 1987)

Shilo, by Phyllis Reynolds Naylor (Yearling, 1992)

Stuart Little, by E. B. White (HarperTrophy, 1974)

The *Captain Underpants* series, by Dav Pilkey (Little Apple, 1997)

The *Hardy Boys* series, by Franklin W. Dixon (Grosset & Dunlap)

The Little Prince, by Antione De Saint-Exupery (Harcourt Brace, 1982)

The *Nancy Drew* series, by Carolyn M. Keene (Platt & Munk)

The Phantom Tollbooth, by Norton Juster (Random House, 1993)

Where the Red Fern Grows, by Wilson Rawls (Bantam Starfire, 1984)

BOOKS BY SUBJECT

Reading/Language Arts

100 Authors Who Shaped World History, by Bill Yenne (Bluewood, 1996)

I'm in the Spotlight!: A Journal of Discovery for Young Writers, by Mary Euretig (Dream Tree, 1993)

Math

57 Great Math Stories and the Problems They Present, by Debbie Haver
   (Instructional Fair, 1998)
Albert Einstein: Physicist and Genius, by Joyce Goldenstern (Enslow, 1995)

Foreign Language

Cinco de Mayo: Yesterday and Today, by Cristina Urritia (Groundwood, 1999)
French Bilingual Dictionary: A Beginner's Guide in Words and Pictures, by
   Gladys C. Lipton (Barron's, 1998)

Computers

101 Things to Do with Your Computer, Gillian Doherty (EDC, 1998)
Bill Gates, by Jeanne M. Lesinski (Lerner, 2000)

Science

1 Day in the Tropical Rainforest, by Jean Craighead George (Ty Crowell, 1990)
Mr. Wizard's Supermarket Science, by Don Herbert (Random House, 1980)

Social Studies

Children's History of the 20th Century (DK, 1999)
How the U.S. Government Works, by Syl Sobel (Barron's, 1999)

Music/Arts

Illustrated Book of Ballet Stories, by Barbara Newman (DK, 1997)
The Magic Flute, by Anne Gatti (Chronicle, 1997)

MAGAZINES

The following list of magazines covers a variety of topics and reading levels. Included is a synopsis of content.

Chickadee Magazine, How-to, personal experience

Children's Playmate, articles with health, sports, fitness, and nutrition themes

Crayola Kids Magazine, crafts, puzzles, and activities

Hopscotch: The Magazine for Girls, covers pets, crafts, hobbies, games, science, fiction, history, puzzles

Jack and Jill, articles, stories, and activities with health, safety, exercise, and nutrition themes

Owl Magazine: The Discovery Magazine for Children, personal experience, photo features, science and environmental features

Ranger Rick, articles relating to nature, conservation, the outdoors, environmental problems, or natural science

Sports Illustrated For Kids, games, general interest, humor, how-to, photos, inspirational

Time for Kids, current events, photos

U.S. Kids, A Weekly Reader Magazine, general interest, how-to, interview, science, computers, multiculturalism

WEBSITES

At the time of publication, the websites listed here were current. Due to the ever-changing nature of the web, we cannot guarantee their continued existence or content. Parents should always supervise their children while they are on the Internet.

If you have concerns and you would like to know more about Internet safety, visit the FBI's site "A Parent's Guide to Internet Safety," at www.fbi.gov/library/pguide/pguide.htm; or you can try www.ed.gov/pubs/parents/internet for "Parents Guide to the Internet," which is hosted by the U.S. Department of Education.

Homework Help

Homework is not likely to be listed among your child's favorite pastimes. The sites below are a great way to make homework time less of a challenge.

www.bjpinchbeck.com
   This site, now hosted on Discovery.com, was created by B.J. and his father. This is a great portal to hundreds of sites dedicated to helping students complete their homework, and to learn something new.

www.bigchalk.com
   Formerly HomeworkCentral.com, BigChalk now encompasses resources for students, parents, and teachers. If your child needs help with homework, he can find help that is both grade and subject specific.

Reference Guides

Perhaps for the first time, your third grader will be asked to complete assignments that require some research. The Internet is a great place to gain access to excellent reference sites such as the ones listed below.

www.brittanica.com
   This site offers free access to Britannica Encyclopaedias as well as a wealth of other new reference sites.

http://kids.infoplease.com
   At Infoplease, students not only have access to a homework center, but there are a variety of almanacs, dictionaries, and encyclopedias.

"Edutainment"

By "edutainment," we mean sites that are both educational and entertaining. The goal is that your child will be learning without even knowing it. There are literally hundreds of thousands of great sites for your child to explore. We have tried to bring you a few of the best that not only have great content, but also have excellent links to other sites.

www.crayola.com

The people at Crayola offer a site full of crafts for kids. There is a game room, coloring books, craft suggestions, and stories.

www.exploratorium.edu

The famous San Francisco museum by the same name hosts this site. The museum is dedicated to science, art, and human perception. Here you will find exhibitions from the museum, activities, and resources for projects.

www.funschool.com

Funschool promises regularly updated educational content for children. Click on "Third & Fourth Grade" from the homepage for excellent content developed especially for your child.

http://kids.msfc.nasa.gov

NASA is sure to find some new recruits for the space program from this site! Complete with space art, space stories, and games, this site will keep children captivated for hours.

www.nick.com

This site comes from the folks at Nickelodeon. While much of this site is dedicated to their programming, there are other pages that offer more of a challenge. Go to "Noggin" from the home page to find games and fun facts for children.

http://nyelabs.kcts.org

A must for the budding scientist! *Bill Nye, The Science Guy* has created a site that is a lot of fun for kids. It is loaded with fun and interesting facts and lots of fun and safe to do science projects at home.

www.pbs.org

PBS has a great site for kids, parents, and teachers alike. Head to PBS KIDS from the home page and be astonished by the quality and quantity of content. There are no shortages of great pages from *Sesame Street, Zoom,* and *Arthur.*

Colorful and filled with all your favorite characters, this site is a MUST for parents and kids.

www.surfmonkey.com

The content on this site is sure to please your third grader. Their wonderful links are organized by categories such as playful, artsy, brainy, spacey, newsworthy, techie, worldly, and starstruck.

www.worldbook.com

Head straight for World Book's Fun and Learning page. There you will find games, news and even a Cyber Camp complete with a summer's worth of activities.

www.yahooligans.com

From the creators of Yahoo, come Yahooligans, a web guide designed for children. Topics included are sports, around the world, and arts and entertainment.

SOFTWARE AND CD-ROMs

I F you are hesitant to have your child spend all his free time watching TV or playing video games, computer software and CD-ROMs are an excellent alternative. As technology has improved, so has the quality of children's software. These programs are generally under thirty dollars and can provide hours of fun and educational activities for your child. Software and CD-ROMs can also be a good alternative to the Internet, especially if parents don't have time to monitor all their child's time online. The programs listed below are usually age or grade specific so that your child will be able to use them as refresher activities, or as a booster for subjects in which he is particularly interested.

Reading/Language Arts

READING BLASTER 3RD GRADE

If your child needs help with words, prefixes, suffixes, and sounding out new words, this is a great CD-ROM to purchase. COST: $18.99

CLUEFINDERS READING ADVENTURES AGES 9–12

This CD-ROM teaches children valuable reading comprehension skills, as well as spelling, grammar, and vocabulary. There are also fifty reproducible activities. COST: $15.99

Science

A WORLD OF DINOSAURS

Children who take an interest in science are sure to love this program. There is a dinosaur adventure, as well as a museum. This is a great way to spark interest for those who may be hesitant to consider science a favorite subject. COST: $19.99

I LOVE SCIENCE

This CD-ROM has been designed to pique the interest of seven to eleven year olds, which guarantees that your child can use this program beyond the third grade. There are fun facts, experiments, and exciting locations to keep children interested. COST: $19.99

Social Studies

20TH CENTURY DAY BY DAY

This is a great program to have for your child's reference library. There are thousands of stories, recordings, videos, photos, and biographies to ensure your child's interest in history. COST: $29.95

USA EXPLORER

Your child will have the opportunity to explore U.S. geography and history with this program. There are games, activities, and clues throughout the program which keeps kids thinking and learning while having fun. COST: $17.99

Foreign Language

SMART START SPANISH DELUXE

If you want your child to experience the wonder of speaking another language, this is a great place to start. There is a lesson guidebook, quizzes, sound clips of conversations, as well as vocabulary and grammar instruction. (Also available in other languages.) COST: $29.99

ROSETTA STONE: FRENCH EXPLORER

This CD-ROM is meant to give your child interactive experience with speaking another language. It features native speakers and the instruction can be customized to your child's learning style. This program is available in several different languages. COST: $19.99

Art

CRAYOLA CREATIVITY PACK PRINT FACTORY AND MAKE A MASTERPIECE

Using a variety of tools, your child is encourage to make his own masterpiece. There are reading and writing activities as well as plenty of creative activities. COST: $26.99

HALLMARK CARD STUDIO

This CD-ROM allows children to create their very own greeting cards. There is even a feature that allows children to save addresses, and receive reminders for upcoming holidays. This is a great way to inspire children's creativity, while encouraging them to think of others. COST: $29.99

Math

CARMEN SANDIEGO MATH DETECTIVE

This software comes from the ever-popular *Carmen Sandiego* series. There are different levels of difficulty, a dictionary of math terms, and plenty of hints to help complete math problems. COST: $29.99

MATH ROCK

The skills covered in this CD-ROM range in skill level from first grade to fifth grade, and the topics are just as varied with geometry, logic, patterns and sequences, and basic computation. This is great for children as they develop their ever-increasing math skills. COST: $9.99

TELEVISION PROGRAMMING

IF you are like most households in the United States, you are watching dozens of hours of television every week. Here are some helpful hints:

1. Avoid programs that are geared exclusively toward selling a product.
2. Find programs that have a message, either moral or educational.
3. Talk with your child after watching a program. Discuss the events of the story, how the characters behaved, you can even talk about the commercials they showed.
4. Steer your child to programming that challenges him to think, feel, or communicate. Television should not be time to vegetate.
5. Seek programming that is both educational and entertaining. Believe it or not, there are quality programs out there.

Your third grader may feel he has outgrown such quality programs as *Sesame Street* and *Mr. Rogers' Neighborhood*, in which case, we offer some alternatives. Check your local listings for station and air time.

Bill Nye, The Science Guy
Reading Rainbow
Wishbone
Zoom

Some stations that have plenty of educational programming for children are Animal Planet, The Discovery Channel, The History Channel, The Learning Channel, PBS, and the Travel Channel.

FOR PARENTS

Websites

THERE is a lot to know about your child and her education. For this reason, we would like to offer websites that have content that is both informative and interactive. You can not only read articles about topics of interest, but you can post your own ideas, and ask questions from the experts.

www.about.com

This site, although not dedicated to education and parenting, has a wealth of links on these subjects. The experts at about.com are also there to answer your questions.

www.bigchalk.com

This site is a great resource not only for parents and children, but also for teachers and educators. You can search by subject, grade level, as well as by topic.

www.childfun.com

This site has plenty of tips and resources for parents on every topic as well as a free newsletter with plenty of great ideas for activities for your child.

www.ed.gov

The U.S. Department of Education hosts this site to present accurate and complete information to parents regarding education in the United States. For a more reader-friendly version of the same content, try www.eduhound.com.

www.edu4kids.com

The content on this site is great for parents looking to provide their children with quality, cost-free learning activities in the major subjects.

www.familyeducation.com

This is the best all-around site. It offers information on your child's development through the years, family activities, family news and topics, tips and resources, software downloads, message boards, ideas from parents, and advice from familyeducation.com experts.

www.helpforfamilies.com

This site was developed by a psychologist to help parents handle problems and address issues that children encounter in school.

www.lightspan.com

Lightspan offers plenty of information on education and parenting issues. The site is divided by grade level so you can track your child's progress through the years.

www.parentsoup.com

Parentsoup is not only parent friendly, but also extremely informative. You can search topics arranged by your child's age group, and write to experts on a variety of topics.

Magazines

If your schedule or situation doesn't allow you to do your research on the web, you can have information delivered to your front door. Here are a few of the best parenting magazines we have found.

Family Life Magazine

The mission of this magazine—aimed at the parents of five- to twelve-year-olds—is to help readers "embrace the unique challenges and joys of the busy years when your family is your life."

Offspring Magazine

Offspring, a recent addition to parenting magazines, shows its timeliness by including a heavy element of technology. There are reviews on software and websites, as well as articles on parenting. *Offspring* is published every other month.

Parents Magazine

Parents is one of the best-known monthlies for moms and dads. While this magazine focuses on the early years of your child's life, there are still plenty of relevant articles on older children and education issues.

FOR FURTHER READING

STILL haven't answered all of your questions? There are plenty of books available to the interested parent.

365 Fun-Filled Activities You Can Do with Your Child, by Mary S. Weaver (Adams Media, 1999)

How Is My Third Grader Doing in School?, by Jennifer Jacobson (S&S, 1999)

Little Bit of Everything for 3rd Grade, by Darryl Vriesenga (InstructFare, 1999)

The School Savvy Parent: 365 Insider Tips to Help You Help Your Child, by Rosemarie Clark (Free Spirit, 1999)

What Your Third Grader Needs to Know, by E. D. Hirsch, Jr. (Delta, 1994)